THE MODERN PERIOD: 19

English literature in its historical, cultural and social contexts

Patrick Lee-Browne

Evans Brothers Limited

Published by
Evans Brothers Limited
2A Portman Mansions
Chiltern Street
London W1U 6NR

First published in 2003

Printed in Italy by G. Canale and C. S.p.A. - Turin

British Library Cataloguing in Publication Data

Lee-Browne, Patrick
The Modernist period: 1900-45:
English literature in its historical and social contexts.
(Backgrounds to English literature)
1. English literature - 20th century - History and
criticism - Juvenile literature
2. Great Britain - 20th century - Juvenile literature
I. Title
820.9–00912

ISBN 0237522578

Editors: Nicola Barber, Jinny Johnson
Consultant: Dr James Methven, Lecturer in
English at Oriel College, Oxford
Design: Simon Borrough
Production: Jenny Mulvanny

Acknowledgements

Title page: Poetry/Rare Books
                  Collection/University of Buffalo
     p.9: Topham Picturepoint
     p.13: the art archive
     p.21: Topham Picturepoint
     p.27: The Bridgeman Art Library
     p.33: (top) Hulton Getty
             (bottom) Hulton Getty
     p.41: (top) Corbis
             (bottom) Poetry/Rare Books
             Collection/ University of Buffalo
     p.49: Topham Picturepoint
     p.51: The Bridgeman Art Library
     p.59: Hulton Getty
     p.69: Hulton Getty

For Daisy and Adam

**For permission to use copyright material,
the author and publisher gratefully
acknowledge the following:**

p.78: 'Our Hunting Fathers' and 'Anthem For St
Cecilia's Day' from *Collected Poems* by W.H.
Auden. By permission of Faber and Faber.

p.63: From *Testament of Youth* by Vera Brittain.
Included by permission of her literary executors
Mark Bostridge and Rebecca Williams. Published
by Virago Press.

p.17: 'In Spring Time' by W.H. Davies. By
permission of Mrs H.M. Davies Will Trust.

p.44,56, 81: From 'The Waste Land' and 'Four
Quartets' from *Collected Poems 1909 - 1962* by
T.S. Eliot. By permission of Faber and Faber.

p.28: From *Goodbye To All That* by Robert
Graves, as published by The Penguin Group
(UK). By permission of Carcanet Press Limited.

p.75: From *Brighton Rock* by Graham Greene,
as published by The Penguin Group (UK). By
permission of David Higham Associates.

p.45 - 6, 60, 61: From *Women in Love, The
Rainbow,* and 'Tickets, Please' by D.H.
Lawrence, as published by The Penguin Group
(UK). By permission of Pollinger Limited and the
Estate of Frieda Lawrence Ravagli.

p.72, 76: From *Coming Up for Air* by George
Orwell (Copyright © George Orwell, 1939). By
permission of Bill Hamilton as the Literary
Executor of the Estate of the late Sonia Brownell
Orwell and Secker & Warburg Ltd.

p.53: 'In a Station of the Metro' from *Collected
Shorter Poems* by Ezra Pound. By permission of
Faber and Faber.

p.74: 'Two Armies' from *Collected Poems* by
Stephen Spender. By permission of Faber and
Faber.

p.46, 65, 77 - 78: From *To the Lighthouse,
Orlando,* and *Between the Acts* by Virginia Woolf,
as published by The Penguin Group (UK). World
rights excluding the US granted by the Society of
Authors as the Literary Representative of the
Estate of Virginia Woolf, US rights granted by
Harcourt Brace.

p.30, 36, 61: From 'Easter 1916', 'Sailing to
Byzantium' and 'Coole Park and Ballylee' by W.B.
Yeats. World rights excluding the US granted by
AP Watt Ltd. on behalf of Michael B. Yeats. US
rights granted by Simon and Schuster, Inc.

CONTENTS

1. INTRODUCTION (1900-14)

Beginnings and endings

The end of the Victorian age coincided almost exactly with the end of the 19th century: the great Liberal politician and prime minister, William Gladstone (b.1809), died in 1898; the Labour Representation Committee (renamed the Labour Party in 1906) was founded in 1900; Queen Victoria herself died in 1901; and the Boer War – the last British colonial war before the outbreak of World War I in 1914 – ended in 1902. However, both Queen Victoria's Golden Jubilee in 1887, and her Diamond Jubilee in 1897, were felt by some contemporaries to have marked the beginning of the end of an age. In literary and cultural terms in particular, the last decade of the 19th century was marked by a greater pessimism and realism, which belonged more to the 20th century than to the heady confidence of High Victorian England.

The first half of the 20th century was dominated in historical terms by the two world wars. British domestic history during that period was characterised by the decline of the Liberal Party and its replacement by the Labour Party as the opposition to the Conservatives; by the growth of activity in support of social reform in such areas as women's rights and trade unionism; and by the effects of the Great Depression in America and the rise of Nazi Germany. Up to the outbreak of World War 1 in 1914, English literature and culture in general was largely conservative, looking back to the previous century for its ideas and models. From the 1920s onwards, writers' perceptions and concerns changed. The influence of writers such as James Joyce (1882-1941), Virginia Woolf (1882-1941), D.H. Lawrence (1885-1930) and T.S. Eliot (1888-1965) was to reshape the development of literature through the century. This was also the time when a split began to develop between 'popular' and 'highbrow' or intellectual culture, as forms of mass entertainment such as film, and newspaper and magazine publishing, took hold of the post-war generation.

The political scene

At the end of the 19th century Britain saw itself confidently as the greatest imperial and colonial power in the world, enjoying the trading and cultural links that possession of India, Australia and New Zealand, Canada, South Africa and many other territories brought. World War I did not have the direct impact on the composition of the Empire in the way that World War II did, but the post-war inclusion of the United States in European diplomacy and the realignment of Britain and France as the main European victors of World War 1 (France had been Britain's traditional enemy for

4

centuries) led to a gradual change in perspective about Britain's role in Europe and the world.

The Boer War

In southern Africa, during the late 1880s and '90s, tension rose between the Boer (Dutch) republics of Transvaal and the Orange Free State and the British colonies of Cape Colony and Natal. This was largely a result of the discovery of gold in Transvaal. Cecil Rhodes (1853-1902), the Prime Minister of Cape Colony, worked with the support of the British government to maintain British dominance in southern Africa by confining the Boers to their territory and, where possible, annexing the Boers' land. The Boers were successful in resisting the efforts of Rhodes to take over any of the Transvaal territory, but in 1899 a significant number of British residents living in the Transvaal petitioned Queen Victoria, complaining of maltreatment by the state authorities. Negotiations between Britain and the Boers collapsed and in October 1899 war broke out between the two sides.

In the early stages of the war the Boers had superiority of numbers and equipment. In December 1899, three British armies were defeated in separate encounters and a number of major towns, notably Kimberley, Ladysmith and Mafeking, were besieged. After the top command of the British army was changed, however, Britain gained the ascendant. By October 1900, both the Orange Free State and Transvaal had been occupied and annexed to Britain as colonies. But because many Boers went on fighting as guerrillas, the British government was forced to go on sending more troops to cope with this unexpected turn of events. In order to contain the Boers and deny them the protection of farms and rural communities, the British rounded up the populations of large areas into 'concentration camps', where many died of disease. Over the course of time the British increased their control over the Boers and in March 1902 peace was concluded. As a result of international pressure on Britain, the final settlement was favourable to the Boers: they were given grants to resettle in their devastated farming areas, and British occupation of the Orange Free State and Transvaal was terminated as soon as possible.

Home Rule for Ireland

In 1900, Ireland was a single political region subject to British rule, governed directly by the British parliament in London. There had been an Irish parliament until its abolition in 1800, when the Act of Union brought Ireland into the United Kingdom of Great Britain and Ireland. The British had persuaded the Irish parliament to surrender its sovereignty in the Act of Union by promising political rights to Catholics (who were excluded from taking office), but failed to honour this promise. The political agitation of Daniel O'Connell (1775-1847) and his Catholic Association led to a Bill being passed in 1829 allowing Catholics to sit in Parliament.

Although O'Connell's campaign was an isolated success, the oppression of the Irish by their English landlords, the economic neglect of the country by the British government after the Napoleonic Wars, and the lack of political autonomy all contributed to a growth in Nationalist societies agitating for Irish independence. The Great Famine, caused by the failure of the potato crop in 1845-6, only aggravated the situation, and by the 1870s the 'Irish question' was a major issue in Westminster. A movement calling for Home Rule was established in 1870. Home Rule meant the re-establishment of the Irish parliament to deal with exclusively Irish issues, leaving Westminster to legislate for the United Kingdom as a whole.

The two most prominent figures in this Nationalist movement were Charles Stewart Parnell (1846-91) and Michael Davitt (1846-1906), and in the 1880s and '90s their activities succeeded in making Home Rule the most contentious subject in politics. William Gladstone attempted twice to introduce Home Rule legislation, but the Liberal Party was split in the process and lost power to the Conservatives, who had the support of the House of Lords (which at that time could prevent legislation from being passed) and the strong backing of Irish Protestants. Parnell was involved in a divorce case that destroyed his reputation as a public figure, and by the turn of the century the cause of Irish nationalism seemed to be in the doldrums.

Then, in the early years of the 1900s, the cause found new impetuses. The Gaelic League was formed in 1893 to promote the Irish language (see page 34); in 1905 a Dublin journalist, Arthur Griffith (1872-1922), founded a new political party called Sinn Féin ('We Ourselves') to agitate for the re-establishment of an Irish parliament and to encourage various forms of non-cooperation with British rule; and in 1912 the Liberals introduced another Home Rule Bill to Parliament.

An added complication to the Irish question was the position of Ulster. There had long been a deep divide between the nine predominantly Protestant counties of Ulster in the north and the rest of Ireland, which had always been Catholic. Ulster's religious and cultural background meant that it had close associations with the United Kingdom, and had always provided strong support for the British in the debate about Irish independence. As Home Rule became increasingly likely, Ulster Protestants who wanted to preserve the Union and avoid rule by a Catholic parliament became all the more determined to resist reform and remain subject to the rule of Westminster. Under the leadership of the Unionist politician Sir Edward Carson (1854-1935) they made plans for a provisional government of Ulster to avoid being ruled by a Catholic parliament in

Dublin. While Carson negotiated with the government for Ulster to be excluded from the provisions of the Home Rule Bill, in early 1913 he also set up a resistance army – the Ulster Freedom Force (UFF) – armed with weapons smuggled into the country from Germany and trained by British army officers. A rival volunteer army – called the Irish Volunteers – was promptly formed to counteract the UFF, and was joined by a second force raised by the Irish Republican Brotherhood.

From late 1913 and into 1914 tension mounted steadily: Winston Churchill (1874-1965), who was then First Lord of the Admiralty, ordered part of the British fleet to anchor off Belfast and threatened to bombard the city if Ulster refused to accept Home Rule. By the summer of 1914 it seemed inevitable that civil war would break out. Preparations for armed struggle became more public, and it was only the outbreak of World War I in August 1914 that brought a temporary halt to the slide towards civil war. Although the Home Rule Act was finally passed in September 1914 it was immediately suspended until the war was over. Many Irishmen joined up to fight with the British army, but within Ireland there was no let-up in the preparations of both Catholics and Protestants to defend their respective positions when the opportunity for rebellion arose (see page 30).

The Empire

Britain's success as the greatest trading nation in the world in the mid-19th century was inseparably linked to the size of its empire. British colonies – Canada, India, Australia, New Zealand, South Africa, Uganda, Kenya and many other countries – provided the raw materials for British industry and a domestic market for goods once they had been manufactured. Trade and the opportunity for commercial exploitation were at the heart of Britain's acquisition of new territory, although other motives played a lesser part, such as religious or humanitarian zeal (in the case of David Livingstone's missions into East and Central Africa, for example), or the protection

— THE *TITANIC*—

One reason why Irish Nationalists were keen that Ulster should be included in an independent Ireland was the position of Belfast. Situated in what is now Northern Ireland, Belfast was the second city in Ireland after Dublin and the Nationalists were naturally unwilling to give up such a valuable asset. Belfast's linen and ship-building industries were world-class; the Harland and Wolff shipyard was and is the largest in the city, and it was here that the Titanic was built.

The construction of the Titanic was begun in March 1909 and the ship was completed in early 1912. On the night of 14-15 April 1912 the Titanic collided with an iceberg in the North Atlantic, and sank within three hours. Although the Titanic had more than the regulation number of lifeboats, there were only enough for 1178 people, when there were in fact 3511 passengers and crew on board. More than 1500 people drowned in the icy Atlantic waters.

Thomas Hardy (1840-1928) was asked to write a poem to be read at a 'Dramatic and Operatic Matinée' in May 1912 to raise money for the families of the survivors of the disaster. The result was called 'The Convergence of the Twain'. The poem is far from conventional in its sentiments: it suggests an inevitable and fateful mating of two giants – the ship and the iceberg – caused by the arrogance and pride of human kind and the fickleness of the 'Immanent Will', Hardy's name for the irrational and reckless force controlling human activity.

of existing colonies by annexing neighbouring countries (for example Malaysia in 1874 and Burma in 1885 to protect India). In the course of the 19th century Britain reduced its direct rule in the 'old' white colonies by granting them the status of 'dominions': Canada became a dominion in 1867, Australia in 1900 and New Zealand in 1907.

India was treated differently. The country had been run as a commercial enterprise by the East India Company since 1600, with increasing intervention from the 1770s onwards by the British government until the Indian mutiny of 1857-8. From then on the government took direct control of all aspects of India, and this change in its status was symbolically confirmed when Queen Victoria was declared Empress of India in 1876. Although India's role as the commercial power-house of the Empire was slowly declining, it continued to provide profits that compensated for losses building up elsewhere in the Empire, and remained at the centre of Britain's self-image as an imperial nation. Successive governments undertook territorial wars to protect the trade routes to India in the Middle East and around the Cape of Good Hope. The Zulu War (1879) in South Africa; the occupation of Egypt (1882) and Sudan (1880s and '90s) to protect the Suez Canal; and efforts to control Afghanistan against Russian intervention (1878-9) all demonstrate that Britain's imperial instincts were still vigorous and largely unopposed at home. While the Boer War (see page 5) was largely driven by greed for the gold in the Transvaal, the security of the Cape also played a part in Britain's stated objectives in pursuing the war.

By the turn of the century there was a developing ground swell of opposition to Britain's management of its Empire and its diplomatic relations with its imperial rivals. This was partly motivated by the huge expense of the Boer War, the defeats suffered by the British army in the course of the war, and reports of the appalling treatment of the Boers both inside and outside the concentration camps. Other factors included the increased trading

— KIPLING AND THE EMPIRE —

Rudyard Kipling (1865-1936) has long been stigmatised as a defender of the evils of imperialism and a 'jingoistic' supporter of white supremacy in India and Africa. George Orwell (1903-50) dubbed him the 'laureate of Empire', and this reputation has endured because of the Indian settings of many of his short stories and his best-known novel, Kim (1901), and the subject-matter of many of his more well-known poems. Some of Kipling's poetry does unquestionably denigrate other races and cultures, but modern critical work has focused on the variety of narrative voices in his poetry which suggests that his views are less clear-cut and more ambivalent than might at first appear. 'The Settler', written at the end of the Boer War, is clear-cut in its condemnation of the war:

Here, where my fresh-turned furrows run,
And the deep soil glistens red,
I will repair the wrong that was done
To the living and the dead.
Here, where the senseless bullet fell,
And the barren shrapnel burst,
I will plant a tree, I will dig a well,
Against the heat and the thirst.

Here, in a large and a sunlit land,
Where no wrong bites to the bone,
I will lay my hand in my neighbour's hand,
And together we will atone
For the set folly and the red breach
And the black waste of it all;
Giving and taking counsel each
Over the cattle-kraal.

Sir Giles Gilbert Scott,
Liverpool Anglican Cathedral
(1903, completed 1978)

Scott was only 22 when he won the competition to design a new Anglican cathedral for Liverpool. The scale of the building is vast: the largest Anglican cathedral in the world, it is second only to St Peter's, Rome in size. Scott died in 1960, before it was completed. The cathedral was built in the Gothic style, at a time when more modern approaches were beginning to emerge (see page 56). Scott went on to design the red Post Office telephone kiosk (1935), the power stations at Battersea (completed 1933) and Bankside (completed 1960) on the River Thames in London.

powers of the USA, Russia, France and Germany and a greater awareness of the dangers of political and economic isolation. Agitation from the radical and Liberal sections of British society for greater reflection about Britain's position on the world stage coincided with increased political instability at Westminster.

Social reform and the rise of the Labour Party

Throughout the 19th century the Liberals were generally considered to be the party of social reform. The major shifts in society brought about by the Industrial Revolution had created a new set of social problems associated with urban poverty and the inequality of wealth and representation. The Liberals addressed some of these in a range of economic and social legislation (as did the Conservatives under the leadership of Benjamin Disraeli, 1804-81), but as the party became more and more bogged down in the struggles over Home Rule, other groups took up the cause of radical politics.

The most prominent of these groups was the Fabian Society, founded in London in 1883-4. The Fabians' goal was a socialist democratic state, to be achieved through legislation and social evolution, and among its early members were the historians Sidney Webb (1859-1947) and his wife Beatrice (1858-1943), the writers George Bernard Shaw (1856-1950) and H.G. Wells (1866-1946), and the future prime minister Ramsay MacDonald (1866-1937). The Fabian Society was an upper middle-class organisation, made up of intellectuals who passionately wanted to bring about improvements for the workers, who at that time had themselves no direct means of influencing economic or social policy in Parliament.

The trades unions movement, however, was growing all the time. Trades unions had their roots in mutual and co-operative societies set up to provide social security and health insurance for industrial workers. In the course of the 19th century, the unions developed the role of negotiating wages and working conditions on behalf of their members. They also ensured that working class issues were addressed in Parliament, by co-operating with the Liberal Party in industrial areas. By the end of the century, the trades unions realised that they needed direct representation in Parliament rather than relying on their Liberal allies, who had a different set of priorities. The miners' leader and journalist Keir Hardie (1856-1915) became the first MP to represent the working class when he was elected as an independent member in 1892. He was involved in the launching of the Independent Labour Party in the following year, but it was not a success because it lacked widespread support from the unions.

More successful was the Labour Representation Committee (LRC), set up by the Trades Union Congress in 1900. The viability of this new party was immediately recognised by the Liberals, who made an electoral pact with Labour in 1903 to ensure that Labour candidates were given the Liberal vote in constituencies where the vote might be split and so let in a Unionist candidate. In 1906 the LRC changed its name to the Labour Party, and in the general election of that year, the new party already boasted 29 MPs. To start off with, the Labour Party enjoyed limited success because most of the inhabitants of the industrial areas it represented did not have the vote, and the party saw itself chiefly as a trade union pressure group. But the dramatic growth of the party in the next 20 years was proof that such a party had been badly needed in British politics.

Although the Labour Party was reliant on the pact with the Liberals up to 1914, various factors after World War I changed the balance of power dramatically. The party re-organised itself with a proper constitution, structure and objectives, and in 1918 the Representation of the People Act gave the vote to all men over 21 and women over 30. By 1922, the Labour Party was the main opposition in Parliament to the Conservatives, and in 1924 the first Labour government was formed under the leadership of Ramsay MacDonald.

The build-up to war

The instability in Europe that resulted in World War I was created by four main factors. First, Germany, which became a single unified state between 1864 and 1871, rapidly developed as an industrial and imperial competitor to the more established European nations. The increasing German power and influence in central Europe prompted other major European states to create a series of alliances to defend their interests which, in turn, led to increased diplomatic and territorial tension. By the outbreak of war in 1914 Britain, France and Russia formed one alliance, while Germany, Austria-Hungary and Italy formed another. Second, European countries treated Africa as a proving ground for their imperial strength and the 'Scramble for Africa' at the end of the 19th century again led to mutual suspicion and territorial aggression between the major powers. Third, increased nationalism in the Balkan region in particular threatened to destabilise the Ottoman (Turkish) and Austro-Hungarian empires, and with them the rest of the delicately balanced international détente. There was a sequence of military crises in the Balkans from 1870 to the outbreak of World War I. The political response to the last of these, in the summer of 1914, set the two alliances on an unstoppable collision course and was the fourth and final ingredient leading to the declaration of war in August 1914.

Germany had been building up its military resources for 30 years when war broke out, and had a plan already prepared (the

11

'Schlieffen plan') to allow it to fight a war both against Britain and France in the West and against Russia in the East. In 1897 the Secretary of State for the German Navy, Admiral von Tirpitz (1849-1930), had started a programme of major naval expansion to challenge the maritime supremacy that Britain had enjoyed since the Napoleonic Wars at the start of the 19th century. Britain reacted by increasing the rate of production of its own fleet, and by developing a new class of battleship called the *Dreadnought* in 1906. Arms production of all kinds boomed in all the major countries: firms such as Vickers, Krupps, Skoda and Creusot all fuelled the spirit of aggressive competition, and certainly made the war more deadly when it finally broke out. Although by 1914 Britain had preserved its dominance in naval terms, and was spending more on defence than its rival, it was the only major player not to have a conscript army, and possibly the nation with the least motivation to go to war.

Science and technology

Just as Britain became increasingly drawn into the politics of Europe in the opening of the 20th century, so too it became more influenced by the technology and culture of both Europe and the United States. This was partly as a result of World War I, but also because of the growth of art forms associated with popular culture and of ever more rapid forms of communication. The Italian inventor Guglielmo Marconi (1874-1937) started experimenting with radio transmissions in 1894, and by 1899 had successfully communicated from Dover to Calais across the English Channel. In December 1901 he received a transmission in St Johns, Newfoundland sent from Poldhu in Cornwall, and in 1918 he sent the first radio message from England to Australia. This new radio technology had immediate application in navigation and communications, but led to the rapid expansion of broadcasting as well.

Other technologies made their mark on the early 20th century with equal speed. The invention of the internal combustion engine in the 1870s made possible the development of the automobile industry. At the end of the century cars were handmade in small numbers by manufacturers such as Daimler, Benz, Peugeot and Isotta-Fraschini; they were expensive to buy and to maintain. But the increasing sophistication of manufacturing methods in Europe and America meant that the precision-made parts necessary for cars to work reliably could be made relatively cheaply. The American manufacturer Henry Ford (1863-1947) developed the world's first 'assembly line' in his factory in Detroit, making just one or two different models of car which were famously always painted black. The mass-production of the Model T Ford began in 1908 and was

Ellis Martin,
Poster for the Great Western Railway (c.1922)
The railway poster was widely used in the early 20th century to advertise
holiday travel, with images of sandy beaches, sunny weather and simple
family fun. At the same time, the four major railway companies
developed a strong brand image, using everything from locomotives to
leaflet design to reinforce their corporate identity. The Great Western
Railway, for which this poster was produced, capitalised on the popularity
of Devon and Cornwall as popular holiday resorts within a few hours'
travel from London.

immensely successful. By 1920 half the cars in the world were Model Ts, and by 1929 there were over 26 million cars registered in the United States.

Developments in the air mirrored the progress on the ground. The Wright brothers – Orville (1871-1948) and Wilbur (1867-1912) – made the first powered, controlled heavier-than-air flight in 1903, in North Carolina, USA. Although World War I delayed the development of the aeroplane for commercial use, a seaplane service was established in Florida in 1914, and intense development in aeronautical engineering during the war meant that aeroplanes had established themselves as a vital part of military tactics by the end of the war. In 1919, two British pilots, John Alcock and Arthur Whitten-Brown, made the first non-stop transatlantic crossing from St Johns, Newfoundland to Ireland, although it was not until after World War II that commercial transatlantic flights became practical.

Looking back and forwards

Perhaps ironically, in an age of so much technological development and international friction, much of the literature of the first 15 years of the 20th century looked back to the past. Nevertheless, out of it emerged the dominant movement of the early 20th century, Modernism (see Chapter 4). The start of the century is, of course, an artificial starting-point for a period, and in this case divides the working careers of a number of important authors, such as Thomas Hardy, Henry James (1843-1916), Joseph Conrad (1857-1924), Rudyard Kipling, W.B. Yeats (1865-1939) and H.G. Wells, to name only the most well-known.

The two pre-eminent British poets before World War I were Hardy and Yeats (see Chapter 3 for more information on Yeats). In the 19th century Hardy had almost exclusively published novels set in his native Dorset, but after the negative reception of *Jude the Obscure* in 1895 he turned his attention to publishing poetry, which he had been writing since he began his career as an author in the 1870s. 'The Darkling Thrush', written on the last day of the old century, 31 December 1900,

— CINEMA IN THE EARLY—
20TH CENTURY

Cinema started in 1895, when the French inventors Louis and Auguste Lumière showed a series of short films in Paris. The European industry was soon dominated by two French firms, Gaumont and Pathé, both of which established near monopolies by creating agencies and buying up chains of film theatres. While early 20th-century French films were often no more than filmed versions of stage plays, the Italian film industry was responsible for the popularisation of the feature film with early costume blockbusters such as The Last Days of Pompeii *(Luigi Maggi, 1908) and* Quo Vadis? *(Enrico Guazzoni 1912). In the USA, the creation of movie theatres that were cheap and quick to build (called 'nickelodeons' because the price of admission was a nickel – five cents), provided a mass market for the expanding film industry. In 1908 the ten most powerful film-makers in the USA joined together to form the Motion Picture Patents Company (MPPC) in order to control the distribution of their films and prevent illegal copies being made and shown. The American film industry settled on the West coast, in an area called Hollywood, where there was plenty of sunshine for film-making and which was close to spectacular scenery. During World War I, film-making was badly disrupted in Europe, allowing companies in the USA to establish Hollywood as the world centre for cinema.*

typifies Thomas Hardy's bleak outlook on life, acknowledging the Romantic notion of the relationship between Man and Nature, and yet caught between hope and despair at what that relationship might mean:

> So little cause for carolings
> > Of such ecstatic sound
> Was written on terrestrial things
> > Afar or near around,
> That I could think there trembled through
> > His happy good-night air
> Some blessed Hope, whereof he knew
> > And I was unaware.

Henry James and Joseph Conrad

Henry James was born in New York, and by his mid-twenties had earned a reputation as an up-and-coming writer of short stories and reviews. In 1869 he visited Europe for a year, returning in 1875 to live in Paris until 1876, and from then until his death in England. In 1915 he became a naturalised British subject. English upper-class society suited his temperament and provided the atmosphere in which he could write and the relationships that provided the themes for his novels. These examine in different ways the experience of being an American in Europe, and the clash of cultures that accompanies it. Like James himself, his characters are often rootless, floating through the high society across Europe and concerned with money and art.

Another non-native English writer of the early 20th century was Joseph Conrad. He was born in the Ukraine to Polish parents and named Teodor Jozef Konrad Korzeniowski. His parents were living in exile as a result of his father's involvement in nationalist activity against Russian rule in Poland. At the age of 17, Conrad began a career at sea, joining the French merchant navy for four years and subsequently serving in the British merchant marine for 16 years. In about 1883 he started to use English to write letters, and in 1886 he became a British subject.

Joseph Conrad's career at sea ended in 1894, and from then on he turned to writing. Many of his novels drew on the experiences and characters he had encountered at sea in all quarters of the globe. One of his later exploits, working for the Belgian king as captain of a steamboat on the Congo river in Africa in 1889, became the basis of his most well-known work, *Heart of Darkness* (1902). The influence of his father's nationalist activities can be seen in two of his most successful novels, *The Secret Agent* (1907) and *Under Western Eyes* (1911), although it is for the books set at sea that he is best-known.

British theatre

If the style and technique of much early 20th-century literature was still conservative and backward-looking, Victorian theatre was, by and large, dominated by plays that exploited sentimentality and melodrama, and featured conventional plots and characterisation. It was not until the very end of the century that the plays of Oscar Wilde (1854-1900) and, more significantly, George Bernard Shaw started a new direction in British theatre. These two authors – both Irishmen who had settled in England – wrote plays that relied on satirical wit and verbal dexterity, and that were much more unorthodox than their predecessors' in their subject matter and its treatment. In this respect they owed much to the technique of the Norwegian playwright Henrik Ibsen (1828-1906) in striking a balance between providing good dramatic entertainment and presenting the playwright's thoughts and opinions of an abstract nature through dramatic situation and characterisation (see box page 39).

Wilde died in 1900, but Shaw was just beginning his career as a playwright at the turn of the century, upsetting the authorities in the process by his outspoken views and the choice of topics for his plays (for example, *Mrs Warren's Profession*, 1894, was banned from the stage until 1902 because it was about prostitution). By 1914 he was established as a major comic playwright, with a long string of successful plays behind him, focused on various ethical and social issues such as the Irish question, war and pacifism and the role of women in society.

Two other writers of the early 20th century who made their mark on the theatre were Harley Granville-Barker (1877-1946) and John Galsworthy (1867-1933). Granville-Barker was as well known as a director and actor as he was a playwright; he made his mark with *The Voysey Inheritance* (1905) but his later writing failed to match the success of that play. John Galsworthy was a prolific novelist, author of the series of Forsyte novels (1906-29) depicting the lives of a well-to-do Edwardian family, and also a successful if now overlooked playwright. The plays that made his name in the theatre were *Strife* (1909) and *The Skin Game* (1920), both of which use naturalistic techniques to put forward a critique of the prevailing social forces of materialism and the difficulties facing the contemporary middle-class.

—THE GEORGIANS—

Edward Marsh (1872-1953) was a civil servant (he served for many years as Winston Churchill's private secretary) with an interest in contemporary art and literature. Marsh built up a large private collection of art and edited a series of five anthologies called Georgian Poetry, *published between 1912 and 1922. Named after King George V (reigned 1910-36), the series was intended to signal the beginning of a vigorous revival in poetry: as Marsh said, 'the new reign [of George V] was itself as new and hopeful as the renaissance in poetry'. Among the poets whose work appeared in the early volumes were W.H. Davies (1871-1940), Wilfrid Gibson (1872-1962), Lascelles Abercrombie (1881-1938) and John Drinkwater (1882-1937). These names may be less well-known today, but others who appeared in* Georgian Poetry *were to acquire greater fame as war poets — Edward Thomas (1878-1917), Siegfried Sassoon (1886-1967), Rupert Brooke (1887-1915), Isaac Rosenberg (1890-1918) and Robert Graves (1895-1985) — or as individual names in their own right — D.H. Lawrence (1888-1935) and Ezra Pound (1885-1972), for example.*

Georgian Poetry *was commercially successful but became associated with a certain kind of English verse: projecting a sentimental view of the countryside, stylistically and formally conventional, and lacking insight or sophistication in its ideas. Some contributors to the early volumes such as Graves, Lawrence and Sassoon fell out with Marsh, and declined to be involved in the last volume of the five.*

'In Spring-Time' by W.H. Davies is representative of the style of Georgian poetry:

> *There's many a pool that holds a cloud*
> *Deep down for miles, to float along;*
> *There's many a hedge that's white with may,*
> *To bring the backward birds to song;*
> *There's many a country lane that smells*
> *Of beanfields, through the night and day:*
> *Then why should I be here this hour,*
> *In Spring-time when the month is May?*
>
> *There's nothing else but stone I see,*
> *With but this ribbon of a sky;*
> *And not a garden big enough*
> *To share it with a butterfly.*
> *Why do I walk these dull dark streets,*
> *In gloom and silence all day long —*
> *In Spring-time, when the blackbird's day*
> *Is four and twenty hours of song.*

17

2. WORLD WAR I (1914-18)

World War I started in August 1914 and ended in November 1918. It was named a 'world war' because it drew so many different nations into conflict as a result of the system of alliances that was one of its causes (see page 11). By the end of the war Great Britain had lost 700,000 dead and 1.6 million wounded; France 1.4 million dead and between 2.5 and 4.25 wounded and Germany 1.7 million dead and 4.2 million wounded. Russia lost 1.7 million killed and 5 million wounded and Austria-Hungary 1.2 million dead and 3.6 million wounded. It should also not be forgotten that the worldwide influenza pandemic that started in March 1918 claimed roughly 27 million lives in the developed world.

In many ways, World War I was the first of two scars that cut right across the 20th century. These left a profound impression on European culture and destroyed much of the sense of continuity that had existed for a century or more in Britain. In literary terms, the war's most immediate legacies are the poetry and the various prose memoirs and accounts of the soldiers who fought in it. But the war also marked a break with the past and provided the opportunity for fresh ideas that saw the arrival of new and challenging works by writers such as Eliot, Joyce and Woolf – not directly reflecting on the war but in other ways affected by it.

Anticipation of war

The outbreak of war in 1914 was preceded by years of anticipation in literature of the conflict between Britain and Germany. As early as 1871, the threat of a German invasion of England had been described in a popular anonymous tale called 'The Battle of Dorking', which appeared in *Blackwood's Magazine*. In 1903, Erskine Childers (1870-1922) published his classic novel *The Riddle of the Sands*, a story that describes how two friends foil a German invasion plot while on a sailing holiday off the Dutch coast. (Childers was an Irish Nationalist who used his yacht to smuggle German guns into Ireland in 1914, fought in the Royal Navy during World War I, joined the IRA and was executed by the Irish Free State authorities in 1922.) A particularly successful evocation of the imminent conflict was written by William Le Queux (1864-1927) called 'The Invasion of 1910', and serialised in the *Daily Mail* in 1905. The following year it sold over a million copies when published in book form. *When William Came; A Story of London under the Hohenzollerns* was published by Saki (the pen-name of H.H. Munro, 1870-1916), in 1913, and imagined a Britain occupied by the Germans, the King and the Tory party having fled to Delhi. The creator of Sherlock Holmes, Sir Arthur Conan Doyle (1859-1930) wrote to the *Fortnightly Review* in 1913 to warn of

the risk of a blockade of Britain by enemy submarines – a tactic
that the Germans were to use almost successfully in 1917, but
his fears were ridiculed by naval experts. He based one of his short
stories, 'Danger!' (1918) on this prediction.

Not everyone was entirely hostile towards Germany and its
ambitions. In *The Riddle of the Sands*, the hero, Davies, reflects on
Germany's global position with admiration and respect, referring to:

> 'the strength and wisdom of her rulers, her dream of a
> Colonial Empire... our great trade rival of the present, our
> great naval rival of the future, she grows and strengthens
> and waits, an ever more formidable factor in the future of
> our delicate network of Empire, sensitive as gossamer to
> external shocks... and we aren't ready for her.'

In *The War in the Air* (1908), H.G. Wells anticipated that air
power would become the decisive factor in the next war, and
described a Europe left in ruins by bombardment from airships.
But if in that book he predicted what a catastrophic effect war
with Germany would have, in 'The War that Will End War' (1914) –
a collection of articles and essays – he betrayed the kind of
nationalistic hatred of Germany that had contributed to the war in
the first place: 'Never had any state in the world so clamoured for
punishment... Every sword that is drawn against Germany now is
a sword drawn for peace.'

George Bernard Shaw was able to look more dispassionately
at the situation in *Common Sense about the War* (1914). Having
ascertained that the German word 'Junker', which was a vogue word
with which to disparage the Germans, meant no more than 'country
gentleman', he observed that this was a war of one group of
country gentlemen against another: 'So let us have no more
nonsense about the Prussian wolf and the British lamb... we cannot
shout for years that we are boys of the bulldog breed and then
suddenly pose as gazelles.' Shaw's views were unpopular, and his
status as an eminent man of letters took a major blow.

Attitudes to war

The imminence of war was met with mixed feelings in Britain. Some
people were enthusiastic at the prospect of fighting Germany, but
as Niall Ferguson shows in his book *The Pity of War* (1998), many
voices called for caution and predicted disaster. A leader in the
Herald, a socialist newspaper, on 30 July 1914 declared:

> Hurrah for War!... Hurrah for blood and entrails, for lungs shot
> through, for weeping mothers and fatherless children, for death
> and disease abroad and destitution at home.

Vera Brittain (1893-1970), who served as a nurse in the war and recorded her experiences in *Testament of Youth* (1933), wrote that on 3 August: 'the events in the newspaper seemed too incredible to be taken seriously.' John Galsworthy (see page 16) wrote on the same day: 'I hate and abhor war of all kinds, I despise and loathe it. And the thought of the million daily acts of its violence and hateful brutishness keeps riving my soul.'

Once the country was engaged in the war the media campaign to influence popular opinion and gain approval for the war began, and poetry was a common means to this end. *The Times* published a number of patriotic poems in the period immediately after 4 August 1914. For example, Robert Bridges (1844-1930) wrote 'Wake Up, England' which appeared on 8 August:

Much suffering shall cleanse thee:
But thou through the flood
Shalt win to Salvation,
To Beauty through blood.

Up, careless, awake!
Ye peacemakers, Fight!
ENGLAND STANDS FOR HONOUR.
GOD DEFEND THE RIGHT!

Propaganda

The enthusiasm of the press for war was reinforced by the work of a committee set up by the government to co-ordinate the efforts of well-known writers in support of the war. Until the entry of the USA into the war in 1917, all official government propaganda was in fact directed abroad, particularly at the United States, in order to sway foreign opinion. The Foreign Secretary had overall responsibility for propaganda, which was divided into news and comment. 'News' was handled by the Foreign Office and the Home Office depending on its nature, while 'comment' was the responsibility of a new body set up by the government, called the Secret War Propaganda Bureau, which was based at Wellington House in London. The Bureau included among its contributors J.M. Barrie (1860-1937; the author of *Peter Pan*), Arnold Bennett (1867-1931), Robert Bridges, Sir Arthur Conan Doyle, John Galsworthy, Thomas Hardy, John Masefield (1878-1967) and H.G. Wells. George Bernard Shaw was the most prominent author who refused to have anything to do with the Bureau. 'Comment' included any kind of information – written or visual – about the war which had the effect of promoting an understanding of Britain's position in and conduct of the war. The Bureau produced individual articles for the press, but also distributed large quantities of pamphlets, books, periodicals and

Frank Hurley,
Endurance in Antarctica, **1915**

Frank Hurley was an Australian photographer who joined the expedition to
the South Pole mounted by Ernest Shackleton, which began in December
1914. Another expedition member described Hurley as 'a warrior with a
camera [who] would go anywhere or do anything to get a picture'. The
expedition had to be abandoned when Shackleton's ship *Endurance* was
caught in pack ice and eventually crushed. Against all the odds
Shackleton succeeded in bringing all the members of the expedition back
to safety. Hurley had to abandon most of his photographic plates, but
kept 120 of the best ones.

news-sheets. Such poems as 'Men who March Away' (1914) by Hardy and 'For all we Have and Are' (1914) by Kipling were early products of the Bureau, and lines from a poem by Laurence Binyon called 'For the Fallen' (1914) – also published as part of the propaganda initiative – have endured to the present in evoking the spirit of national thanksgiving for the soldiers' sacrifice:

They shall not grow old as we that are left grow old:
Age shall not weary them, nor the years condemn.
At the going down of the sun and in the morning,
We will remember them.

Changing attitudes

The work of Rupert Brooke (see box on this page), Julian Grenfell (1888-1915) and Siegfried Sassoon is typical of the early soldier-poets who wrote of the war in terms of honour and duty, with a religious conviction that they were willing to die for their cause. For example, Grenfell's 'Into Battle' (1915) is a song in praise of war: 'The fighting man shall from the sun / Take warmth, and life from the glowing earth.' However, a more realistic and pessimistic perspective took over as the war dragged on through 1915 into 1916, and new voices replaced the early enthusiasts: Ivor Gurney (1890-1937), Wilfred Owen (1893-1918), Isaac Rosenberg, Edward Thomas, and Sassoon, who was now utterly disillusioned by his experiences in the Battle of the Somme in July 1916.

Each poet brought his own background and experiences of war to bear on his work. Sassoon had enjoyed the life of a well-off country family until war broke out, and he brought the fruits of a well-rounded education to bear on his poetic response to the war. Edward Thomas, killed in the Battle of Arras on Easter Monday, 9 April 1917, is widely regarded as one of the foremost war poets, yet he wrote all his poetry in England between December 1914 and January 1917, when he was sent out to France. His work evokes a

— **RUPERT BROOKE** —

One of the most effective pieces of pro-war propaganda was brought about by the death of Rupert Brooke in April 1915, from blood poisoning. Brooke had enjoyed great popularity and success at Cambridge University, and had influential friends such as Winston Churchill and the Prime Minister, Herbert Asquith (1852-1928). Brooke had given Edward Marsh the idea for the first volume of Georgian Poetry *(see box page 17), and worked closely with him on its publication. A sequence of five sonnets called* 1914 *included Brooke's most well-known poem, 'The Soldier' ('If I should die, think only this of me...'), which the Dean of St Paul's Cathedral quoted in his sermon on Easter Sunday, 1915. Brooke's death three weeks later allowed Winston Churchill (the instigator of the Gallipoli offensive towards which Brooke was sailing at the time of his death) to write a fulsome obituary in* The Times. *Brooke became the model of the national soldier-poet, an image that remained strong throughout the war, even though the nature of war poetry changed. The post-war reputations of the more realistic, anti-war poets such as Siegfried Sassoon and Wilfred Owen have risen, but many other poets writing during the war contin-ued to use Brooke as their model. Even by the middle of the war, however, critical voices were raised against the distortion of the truth in such verse. The publisher and critic Arthur Waugh (father of Evelyn Waugh; see page 76) wrote in the* English Review *in December 1916:*

'What strikes the soldier is this. Why does a poet write about a military, a desperate military expedition?... Poets are our strategists, our official "writers up". And this blindness of ours is due to our inexact feeling for words, our hatred of criticism, our refusal to face facts.'

———————

powerful sense of loss and despair even though it is set in the
English countryside and never depicts the war itself. 'Lights Out'
(1916) is one of his most characteristic poems:

> I have come to the borders of sleep,
> The unfathomable deep
> Forest where all must lose
> Their way, however straight,
> Or winding, soon or late;
> They cannot choose...
>
> There is not any book
> Or face of dearest look
> That I would not turn from now
> To go into the unknown
> I must enter, and leave, alone,
> I know not how.
>
> The tall forest towers;
> Its cloudy foliage lowers
> Ahead, shelf above shelf;
> Its silence I hear and obey
> That I may lose my way
> And myself.

Ivor Gurney trained as a musician at Gloucester Cathedral and
the Royal College of Music. He managed to compose songs even
while in the trenches (see box page 26), and music and harmony
are never far from the surface in his work. Isaac Rosenberg was
born into an immigrant Jewish family and was an art student before
the war, familiar with young British artists such as Dora Carrington
(1893-1932) and Stanley Spencer (1891-1959; see page 26).
The influence of his artistic training can be seen in poems such as
'Break of day in the Trenches' (1916), 'Dead Man's Dump' (1917)
or 'Louse Hunting' (1917), from which this extract is taken:

> ...See the silhouettes agape,
> See the gibbering shadows
> Mixed with the battled arms on the wall.
> See gargantuan hooked fingers
> Pluck in supreme flesh
> To smutch supreme littleness.

These well-known 'war poets' had their work published in
newspapers and magazines, or more commonly printed in
collections – for example Gurney's *Severn and Somme* (1917)

or Sassoon's *The Old Huntsman* (1917). But many thousands of soldiers recorded their feelings, experiences and yearnings in poetry, usually written in secret and then sent on in letters to friends at home in England.

The shift from early public enthusiasm to disillusionment and then horror and disgust at the direction and conduct of the war has been well documented. Nevertheless, despite the change of tone and subject matter, war poetry remained essentially conservative in its forms and techniques, and owed little to the developments in the genre that T.S. Eliot and Ezra Pound were working on in the early 20th century. Perhaps unfairly, W.B. Yeats accused Wilfred Owen of being 'all blood, dirt and sucked sugar stick... he calls poets "bards", a girl "a maid" and talks about "Titanic wars"'. In other words, Yeats felt that there was a gap between the subject matter that Owen wrote about and the forms and language with which he did it. Yeats edited the *Oxford Book of Modern Verse* (1936) but left Owen out of the anthology.

Jon Silkin in the Introduction to *The Penguin Book of First World War Poetry* (1979) and *Out of Battle* (1987) links the major war poets to the Romantic poets of the beginning of the 19th century in the way they reacted to the events around them. Owen was strongly influenced by the work of John Keats (1795-1821), for example, and the characteristic rejection of poetic language in Sassoon's satirical poetry is in the tradition of William Wordsworth's (1770-1850) declaration in the Preface to *Lyrical Ballads* (1798) that he wished to write 'in the language of men for men'. In his use of satire, Sassoon was also following in a tradition used by Percy Shelley (1792-1822) in poems such as 'The Mask of Anarchy' (1832).

Paul Fussell in his book *The Great War and Modern Memory* (1975) suggests that although the war poets and other writers used conventional forms, this was because the war was an experience that no one had ever before encountered, and so writers reacted in the best way available – through an ironic treatment of traditional literary forms, including the creation of types of myths and other fantasies. The Angel of Mons, reported to have protected retreating British troops is one example. Another kind, in verse, is Wilfred Owen's 'Parable of the Old Man and the Young', in which he tells the story of Abraham preparing to sacrifice his son Isaac on God's command. At the end of the poem, though, the parable is given a chilling, modern twist:

> Behold,
> A ram, caught in a thicket by its horns;
> Offer the Ram of Pride instead of him.
> But the old man would not so, but slew his son,
> And half the seed of Europe, one by one.

War artists

Isaac Rosenberg was only one of many artists who signed up as active soldiers and who also sometimes found time and material to continue their art in their spare time. But whereas in this case art was a means of keeping in touch with normality and passing the time, it also had another important role. As the war continued into 1916, the Wellington House propaganda department (see page 20) found that the visual image was becoming a more important medium of information. Films and photographs were well-established, but there were relatively few official photographers on the Western Front, and the landscape and visual set-pieces of the war were becoming increasingly familiar and nondescript. As a result, the head of the Wellington House department, C.F. Masterman, decided to finance official war artists to develop a new angle on the presentation of the war effort.

In July 1916 the first official war artist, Muirhead Bone (1876-1953) was sent to France, and he worked on a series of drawings of the Somme offensive. He was joined by a portraitist, Francis Dodd (1874-1947), in December 1916, who was recruited with the task of drawing portraits of the naval and army commanders for newspaper publication. James McBey (1883-1957) was appointed in April 1917 to draw 'appropriate war scenes in Egypt and Palestine for the purposes both of propaganda at the present time and of historical record in the future', and his work includes portraits of T.E. Lawrence (1888-1935; Lawrence of Arabia) and the leaders of the Arab revolt against the Turks in the Hejaz.

Unlike these first three, a number of subsequent war artists had already seen active service before being appointed in their new role. C.R.W. Nevinson (1889-1946) served in the Belgian Red Cross in 1915-6, and had exhibited several war paintings in London in 1916 before being employed as an official artist in the summer of 1917. He had worked with Picasso (1881-1973) and other Cubists (see page 48), had a firm association with Wyndham Lewis (1882-1957) and the Vorticists (see page 50), and collaborated with Filippo Marinetti (1876-1944; see page 48) to establish English Futurism . His early work for the Department of Information (the successor to Wellington House) was considered dull, possibly because he tried too hard to conform. Rejecting the techniques that made his early work so exciting, he turned to a more realistic style that offended the censors by showing corpses and 'unworthy' portraits of private soldiers.

Eric Kennington (1888-1960) had served with the London Regiment until June 1915, when he was injured. Like Nevinson, he had exhibited privately during the war, and was subsequently employed as an official artist in August 1917. He worked in pastels, which did not lend itself to easy handling or reproduction, but his portraits of ordinary soldiers and the conditions of everyday life are among the most evocative of all the official paintings. Paul Nash (1889-1946) had enjoyed a strong critical reputation before the war, and although it was thought by some in the Department of Information that his style was 'not what the British public generally will like', his paintings of Flanders during the last days of the Third Battle of Ypres (Passchendaele) in October 1917 are among the most intense and provocative by any of the official artists.

Another important pre-war artist, Stanley Spencer, was engaged in active service in Macedonia (Greece) for the second half of the war and was only released from the ranks in December 1918. Nevertheless, he considered the time spent in Macedonia to be a preparation, rather than a waste of time, and his experiences in the war were to find an outlet in his painting of the murals (1927-32) in the Sandham Memorial Chapel at Burghclere in his native Berkshire. This chapel was built as a memorial to a soldier who had died of an illness caught in Macedonia, and Spencer used the sketches made as an official artist immediately after the war as the basis of his work.

In March 1917 the Imperial War Museum (IWM) was founded. Its earliest purpose was to organise touring exhibitions which tied in closely to the work of the Department of Information. From the outset, the IWM also began to build up a collection of exhibits and records of the war while these were still readily accessible, and the friendly relationship between the IWM and the Department of Information meant that a large number of the official artists' pictures, and many others besides, were acquired by the museum. An exhibition of official artists' work was mounted at the Royal Academy of Art in London in December 1919, and although it was generally well-received by the art critics, the popular press was outraged at the *avant-garde* quality of many of the exhibits and questioned the patriotism and politics of the exhibition.

—— COMPOSERS OF—— WORLD WAR I

In musical terms, World War I is often associated with music-hall songs such as 'It's a Long Way to Tipperary' or 'Keep the Home Fires Burning', which were used by the soldiers as marching songs or as expressions of community and togetherness. Parody and satire are age-old weapons of troops against their superiors as a way of making conditions bearable, and a number of the well-known songs — 'No more soldiering for me' or 'I don't want to be a soldier', for example — are parodies of hymn tunes or popular tunes by contemporary composers.

A number of classically trained composers joined the armed forces. George Butterworth (1885-1916) had been active in the revival of traditional English folk music led by Cecil Sharp (1859-1924) and Ralph Vaughan Williams (1872-1958; see page 27). He was killed in the Somme offensive in August 1916. W. Denis Browne (1888-1915) was a friend of Rupert Brooke from school days. His interest in music developed while at university, and although he was killed in June 1915 during the Gallipoli campaign having only just begun his career (he was 27), the music that he left behind him indicated real talent. Ivor Gurney (see page 23) had studied at the Royal College of Music just before the war, and had already created a distinctive musical voice by the time he was drafted into the army in 1915. He managed to write five high-quality songs while in the trenches, including the only setting he made of his own poetry, 'Severn Meadows'. He was wounded and gassed, and invalided back to England in 1917. He is now regarded as a significant song composer as well as one of the major war poets. Although he battled unsuccessfully with mental illness from 1920 until his death in 1937, he still managed to write songs and poetry during that period, though with increasing lack of control or success.

———————————

Jacob Epstein,
Head of Ralph Vaughan Williams (1950)
Epstein was one of the leading portrait sculptors of the 20th century.
Vaughan Williams played a central role in the revival of English
'nationalistic' music from the turn of the century onwards. The influence
of traditional songs and folk music, as well as the music of the Tudor
period, runs deep through his musical style.

Prose responses to the war

A number of writers who had made a poetic response to their experiences during the fighting chose to write about the war at greater length in prose after the event. These included Robert Graves's *Goodbye to all That* (1929, rewritten 1957), Edmund Blunden's (1896-1974) *Undertones of War* (1928), and Siegfried Sassoon's *Memoirs of a Fox-Hunting Man* (1928) and *Memoirs of an Infantry Officer* (1930). *Goodbye to all That* is a satirical record of Graves's war, written in three months, and is constructed around a series of sketches that stress the absurdity and farce of the war, focusing on the human element of the experience rather than the landscape or the day-to-day progress of the war itself. Graves and Sassoon both served in the same regiment, the Royal Welch, and *Goodbye to all That* describes Graves's friendship with the other poet. The following anecdote is typical of Graves's style and laconic approach:

> Two young miners, in another company, disliked their sergeant, who had a down on them and gave them all the most dirty and dangerous jobs. When they were in billets he crimed them for things they hadn't done; so they decided to kill him. Later, they reported at Battalion Orderly Room and asked to see the adjutant...The adjutant happened to see them and asked: 'Well, what is it you want?'
> Smartly slapping the small-of-the-butt of their sloped rifles, they said: 'We've come to report, sir, that we're very sorry, but we've shot our company sergeant-major.'
> The adjutant said: 'Good heavens, how did that happen?'
> 'It was an accident, sir.'
> 'What do you mean, you damn fools? Did you mistake him for a spy?'
> 'No, sir, we mistook him for our platoon sergeant.'
> So they were both court-martialled and shot by a firing squad of their own company against the wall of a convent at Béthune. Their last words were the battalion rallying-cry: 'Stick it, the Welch!...' The French military governor was present at the execution, and made a little speech saying how gloriously British soldiers can die.

Paul Fussell describes Edmund Blunden's *Undertones of War* as 'an extended pastoral elegy in prose'. The book is more consciously literary than Graves's, drawing on a range of authors and written in a style that appears to make light of his experiences, but draws attention to the uncivilised nature of war by describing it in elegant, Classical terms. He originally entitled the book *De Bello Germanico* '[Concerning] the German War' – a parody of Caesar's record of his own campaigns in France in *De Bello Gallico*:

The position grew no better during the night, and the succeeding day was dismal, noisy and horrid with sudden death. Tempers were not good, and I found myself suddenly threatening a sergeant-major with arrest for some unfriendly view which he was urging on the headquarters in general. Then, there were such incidents as the death of a runner called Wrackley, a sensitive and willing youth, just as he set out for the companies; intercepted by a shrapnel bullet, he fell on one knee, and his stretched-out hand still clutched his message.

The book ends with the image of Blunden himself as 'a harmless young shepherd in a soldier's coat', and contains after the main text a 'Supplement of Poetical Interpretations and Variations': a series of 31 poems written after the war had ended which link the fighting to the countryside in which it was taking place. It is a less realistic treatment than Graves's but just as individual.

Siegfried Sassoon wrote an autobiographical trilogy recording his life up to the end of the war in 1918, called *The Memoirs of George Sherston*. The first volume, *Memoirs of a Fox-Hunting Man*, describes his growing up in a wealthy family in Kent, and joining the army in 1914. The last part of the book treats his early experiences on the Western Front, ending on Easter Sunday. *Memoirs of an Infantry Officer* and *Sherston's Progress* (1936) cover the remainder of the war, including Sassoon's turning against the Establishment which he had so wholeheartedly supported up to and at the outbreak of the war. His friendship with Graves ('David Cromlech') and the time spent recovering from shell-shock at Craiglockhart Hospital in Edinburgh are prominent features of these two volumes.

An interesting pair of novels was written by the husband and wife team of Richard Aldington (1892-1962) and Hilda Doolittle (1886-1961). Aldington was a poet and novelist who suffered the effects of gas and shell-shock. In 1929 he published *Death of a Hero*, a novel based largely on his own experiences before and during the war in which he took the opportunity to satirise the artistic circles in which he moved in London, and to paint a negative picture of the increasingly strained relationship with his wife. Nevertheless, the book was highly successful, and ranks alongside the work of Sassoon and Graves as a record of the war.

Hilda Doolittle (known as 'HD') was an American poet, a colleague and former fiancée of Ezra Pound who was closely involved in the Imagist movement (see page 52). Her novel *Bid Me to Live* (1960) is her own deeply moving version of her wartime experiences in London.

3. IRELAND

The Easter Rising

The outbreak of World War I brought with it a temporary lull in the heated political manoeuvring over Irish independence, partly because the Home Rule Bill was finally put on the statute book (see page 5) and partly because the British government was preoccupied with the war against Germany. However, in 1916 the Irish Republican Brotherhood (IRB) decided to capitalise on the situation; and made plans with the nationalist group the Irish Volunteers (see page 7) for an armed rising on Easter Sunday, 24 April. The IRB was in contact with the German high command, and arranged for arms to be smuggled into Ireland on the Thursday before the rising. But the plans went hopelessly awry, and although a German ship arrived at the agreed rendezvous, no one was there to meet it. Deciding that the operation could not succeed without German arms, the Commander in Chief of the Irish Volunteers put coded advertisements in the papers cancelling the rebellion, but two commanders of local volunteer forces decided to go ahead anyway.

On Easter Monday, members of the Irish Volunteers took over the General Post Office and other strategic buildings in the middle of Dublin, and proclaimed the creation of the Irish Republic. The British army moved in to put down the rebellion, and after a week of sporadic street fighting and artillery bombardment by the British, the rebels surrendered on 29 April. The leaders and signatories of the proclamation of the Republic were given a summary court-martial. In the course of the following week, 15 of the rebels were executed. One of the leaders of the uprising, Eamon de Valera (1882-1975), was sentenced to death but was spared at the last minute. Although there was little real popular support for the Easter Rising from the country at large – the rebels were jeered by onlookers as they emerged from the Post Office – the speed and callousness of the British response created a mood of revulsion among the Irish. The executed rebels quickly became martyrs and their treatment helped to fuel the civil unrest that remained until the declaration of the Irish Free State in 1921.

— 'EASTER 1916' —

W.B. Yeats responded to the Easter Rising with a terse, moving poem that contrasts a human picture of the patriots and Nationalists before the Rising with a complex description of the heroism created by the martyrs' deaths:

> *We know their dream; enough*
> *To know they dreamed and are dead;*
> *And what if excess of love*
> *Bewildered them till they died?*
> *I write it out in a verse —*
> *MacDonagh and MacBride*
> *And Connolly and Pearse*
> *Now and in time to be,*
> *Wherever green is worn,*
> *Are changed, changed utterly;*
> *A terrible beauty is born.*

The War of Independence

In the course of 1917, support for Sinn Féin (see page 6) grew across Ireland as a direct result of the Easter Rising and its harsh aftermath. The party won seats in four by-elections and orchestrated large public demonstrations and shows of strength that went on into 1918. In that year the British government introduced a Bill introducing conscription to Ireland, something that had previously been avoided as too politically sensitive. The entire spectrum of Irish politics was united against the Bill, and a general strike in opposition to conscription brought the country to a standstill on 22 April.

In the general election in December 1918 the Nationalist Home Rule Party, which had been the primary force in Irish politics for over 35 years, lost heavily to Sinn Féin. In all, 73 Sinn Féin members were elected as members of the Westminster parliament. This was the first election in which women were allowed to stand as candidates and to vote, and one of the new Sinn Féin MPs was W.B. Yeats's friend, Constance Gore-Booth, Countess Markievicz (1868-1927). However, she was unable to take her seat in the House of Commons as she was in prison following her part in the Easter Rising, and so Lady Nancy Astor (1879-1964), who was elected in a by-election in Plymouth in 1919, had the distinction of being the first woman to sit in the House of Commons.

The pressure on the British government continued into 1919. In January, Sinn Féin set up an Irish National Assembly, or Dáil Eireann, the first time a representative assembly had met in Ireland since 1800. A cabinet was elected, a constitution for the Dáil drawn up, and a Declaration of Independence issued, but neither London nor Dublin took the new body too seriously, since it had no real power. Nevertheless, the establishment of the Dáil signalled that Sinn Féin remained committed to a political resolution to the conflict with the British government, even though military factions such as the Irish Republican Army (IRA; the successor to the IRB) were increasing their attacks on arms stores and creating public disobedience wherever possible. The British government responded to the growing number of attacks with greater violence, which served only to increase the Irish determination to be rid of the British. De Valera left Ireland for America in June 1919, to raise funds among the many emigrant Irish communities there, convinced that a political settlement was the only way forward.

In De Valera's absence, another Assembly leader called Michael Collins (1890-1922) drove the country towards armed rebellion, both against the British and against Irish members of the Royal Irish Constabulary (RIC; the national police force) and other 'collaborators'. Significant numbers of RIC members left the force, and so from the beginning of 1920, the RIC began to recruit in

England, drawing on battle-hardened ex-servicemen who had fought in World War I to police a nation with which they had no sympathy. These English policemen were known as the 'Black and Tans' – the name seems to have come from a pack of hounds near where an RIC unit operated in County Tipperary – and the ruthlessness and brutality with which they carried out the task of imposing order and punishing Republican activity meant that they were hated and feared by the whole population. Once again, this only served to increase popular support for the Nationalist cause.

In the spring and summer of 1920 the IRA stepped up its guerrilla tactics in the countryside, and democratic law and order effectively broke down in many areas of Ireland. Yet it was clear that neither side was going to win the 'War of Independence', as it was known, by a military solution, since the IRA's guerrilla tactics were too well-established, and resistance to British rule was too widespread to be effectively policed. However, political negotiations were not straightforward, since although the British prime minister, David Lloyd George (1863-1945) announced in April 1921 that he would meet representatives of the Irish people, he was not prepared to negotiate with men such as Collins, whom he had described publicly as a murderer. Nor was Lloyd George willing to consider a completely independent Ireland, insisting that Ulster be treated separately from the rest of the country.

Nevertheless, in 1921 a delegation from the Dáil which included Collins and Arthur Griffith (see page 6) signed a treaty with the British government. The treaty established Ireland as a dominion, with the same self-governing status as, for example, Canada or Australia. The new dominion was to be called the Irish Free State. Ulster, to be known from then on as Northern Ireland, was excluded from the new state. As part of the treaty, members of the Dáil were required to swear an oath of allegiance to the Crown. Although the Dáil recognised the treaty, De Valera was unable to accept its terms and left the Dáil. A split between the provisional government under Collins and Griffith and the anti-treaty Republicans led to two years of bitter civil war in Ireland.

In April 1923, peace between the two sides was declared. De Valera formed a new political party, which was called Fianna Fáil ('Soldiers of Destiny'), and in 1927 he was forced to take the oath of allegiance in order to re-enter parliament. In 1932 Fianna Fáil won sufficient seats for De Valera to form a new government, one of his first acts being to abolish the oath of allegiance. In 1937, De Valera presented a new constitution which abolished the authority of the Crown and replaced the office of governor-general with an elected president. The first holder of that office was Douglas Hyde (1860-1949), the founder of the Gaelic League (see page 34) back in 1893.

The ruins of the General Post Office, Easter 1916

The siege of the GPO in Dublin was an enduring Republican symbol of the Easter Rising in 1916. The building was besieged by British soldiers for six days before its occupants surrendered.

Eamon De Valera at a public meeting in Los Angeles, December 1919

This photograph was taken during De Valera's visit to the United States from June 1919 to January 1920. The purpose of the trip was to raise American funds and goodwill for the Irish independence movement.

The Irish literary renaissance

From the start of the political struggle for Irish independence in the 19th century (see page 5), there was a parallel broader movement campaigning for the revival of a national Irish cultural identity. In 1879, Michael Davitt (see page 6) established the Land League. The aim of this organisation was to fight for various rights for the Irish peasantry, for example the right to fair rents, the right to remain on the land and not to be evicted at will, and the right to sell their tenancies on to whomever they wished. But the Land League also promoted a mythical image of Irish peasants as a dignified and independent people, proud of their country and its way of life, who gave Ireland a distinct character and virtue. According to this idealistic picture these peasants had owned their own land in the times before the English settlers arrived – in fact, they had been just as oppressed by the leading families of Celtic Ireland as by the English.

The Land League had a brief period of success in lobbying for legislation to restrict various landlords' privileges before it was suppressed by the British government in 1881. Nevertheless, the mythology promoted by the Land League held much appeal for Irish writers and artists looking for a symbol of national identity, even though they may not have been overly interested in the actual politics of the situation. It was therefore natural that they should depict native Irish life in their writing.

The Gaelic League was founded in 1893 under the presidency of the writer Douglas Hyde, with the aim of restoring interest in the Irish language – Gaelic – and the history and folklore with which it was associated. The members of the Gaelic League wrote in Gaelic to revive it as a vehicle of literature. At the same time, writers such as George Moore (1852-1933), J.M. Synge (1871-1909) and Yeats were developing a dramatic style in prose and verse that reflected the spoken English of the Irish people, and which would be accessible to the Dublin audiences of their work.

—Eɴɢʟɪsʜ ᴠɪᴇᴡs ᴏғ ᴛʜᴇ Iʀɪsʜ—

For centuries, the English presented the Irish people as illiterate and savage. References in William Shakespeare's (1564-1616) plays, for example, are never complimentary. In Richard II, *Richard declares:*

> *Now for our Irish wars:*
> *We must supplant those rough rug-headed kerns,*
> *Which live like venom where no venom else,*
> *But only they, have privilege to live.*

The 18th-century satirist, Jonathan Swift (1667-1745) was outraged at the practices of Anglo-Irish landlords. His satire A Modest Proposal *(1729) takes the form of a letter from an entrepreneurial gentleman offering a solution to the problem of overpopulation and economic deprivation in Ireland: farm the babies of the peasants as edible delicacies for the rich, thereby reducing the number of beggars, providing tasty meat all year round, and a source of income to Irish mothers.*

Just over 100 years later, in 1836, the novelist and Conservative politician Benjamin Disraeli wrote to The Times: *'The Irish hate our free and fertile isle. They hate our order, our civilisation, our enterprising industry, our sustained courage, our decorous liberty, our pure religion. This wild, reckless, indolent, uncertain and superstitious race have no sympathy with the English character. Their fair ideal of human felicity is an alternation of clannish broils and coarse idolatry. Their history describes an unbroken circle of bigotry and blood.'*

A number of writers produced collections of folk tales and myths, and among the more influential of these were two volumes of saga material, *Cuchulain of Muirthemne* (1902) and *Gods and Fighting Men* (1904) collected by the writer Lady Augusta Gregory (1852-1932; see page 36). These volumes provided the material for Yeats's sequence of plays about the hero Cuchulain, as well as plays based on the legend of Deirdre by George Russell (1867-1935), Synge and Yeats, and Moore's *Diarmuid and Grania* (1901).

Just as the Land League had raised the profile of the Irish peasant for political purposes, the literary revival took the same figure to embody the national culture. Yeats's short play *Cathleen ni Houlihan* (1902), and Synge's plays set on the Aran islands (see page 37), presented audiences with a setting and subject matter that was entirely new to them. English drama was moving towards a more naturalistic technique under the influence of Ibsen (see box page 39), but the influence of myth and folklore meant that Irish theatre at the turn of the century was more figurative (using stock characters and symbolic language and situations) and anti-realistic.

W.B. Yeats

The writer most strongly identified with the revival of Irish culture through literature is William Butler Yeats. Although born in Dublin into a family from Sligo in the northwest of Ireland, Yeats spent most of his childhood and early manhood in London. He made friends with a number of influential writers and thinkers associated with emerging Irish nationalism, including the poet and editor George Russell (known as 'AE'), the Fenian leader John O'Leary (1830-1907), the poet Katharine Tynan (1861-1931), and George Bernard Shaw. In his twenties he became interested in Buddhism, Spiritualism, theosophy and the occult, which were to influence his writing throughout his life. These interests complemented his fascination with Irish fairy tales, legends and stories of the supernatural, and his early poetry drew heavily on such material for its themes and style. At this time Yeats also compiled Irish folklore in several collections, the best-known of which, *The Celtic Twilight* (1893) gave its name to the Irish literary revival. During this first phase of his development as a poet, Yeats was self-consciously Romantic in his style and subject matter, blending myth and folklore with the conventional themes of love and loss.

In 1891 Yeats met and fell in love with the actress Maud Gonne (1865-1953). She was deeply committed to Irish independence, and although she was happy to use the poetic outpourings that his passion provoked in the nationalist cause, she was not interested in returning his love, and rejected his proposals of marriage several times. Yeats's early play *The Countess Cathleen* (1891) was inspired by Maud Gonne, and many of the poems in his romantic collection *The Wind Among the Reeds* (1899) were addressed to her.

Another influential woman whom Yeats met at this time was Lady Augusta Gregory, a playwright and activist in the literary revival. She owned Coole Park, commemorated in Yeats's poem 'The Wild Swans at Coole', and her collaboration with Yeats and the playwright Edward Martyn (1859-1923) led to the creation of the Irish Literary Theatre. This was a theatrical society dedicated to the performance of Irish drama, which in turn was succeeded by the Abbey Theatre, a repertory theatre in Dublin started up in 1904 and committed to the same cause. Yeats produced a number of plays for the Abbey Theatre, as well as several volumes of poetry including *In the Seven Woods* (1903) and *The Green Helmet* (1910).

The second phase of his poetic career saw Yeats becoming more involved in Irish nationalism. He had not been particularly committed to the political or military struggle for Irish independence, but after the Easter Rising of 1916 he was inspired by the execution of the leaders of the rising to write one of his finest poems, 'Easter 1916' (see box page 30). Although his interest in symbolism and mysticism was as strong as ever, he worked it into his poetry – in volumes such as *The Wild Swans at Coole* (1919) and *Michael Robartes and the Dancer* (1921) – without making his writing obscure.

In 1917, Yeats was again refused when he proposed marriage to Maud Gonne. A proposal to Maud's adopted daughter, Iseult, was also turned down. But later that year he was accepted by Georgiana Hyde-Lees, an English lady. The couple lived in England for a while, then restored a Norman tower at Ballylee, where they spent the summers. In 1921, the Irish Free State was created, and Yeats was appointed as a senator in the new parliament. In the following year he was awarded the Nobel Prize for Literature.

— YEATS AND CLASSICAL — MYTHOLOGY

Yeats was open to the influence of a wide range of cultures beyond Irish mythology. He experimented with the traditions of the Japanese Noh theatre, he was excited by being introduced to the work of the Indian poet Rabindranath Tagore (1861-1941), and he became a close friend of the American poet Ezra Pound (see page 54). The Homeric legends of the Trojan Wars, and in particular the figure of Helen of Troy, had a lasting and powerful influence on his work. One of his most well-known poems, 'Sailing to Byzantium', written in 1926, evokes the yearning for a mythical past that has little to do with the Irish folk heroes Cuchulain or Finn MacCool:

That is no country for old men. The young
In one another's arms; birds in the trees,
– Those dying generations – at their song;
The salmon-falls, the mackerel-crowded seas,
Fish, flesh or fowl, commend all summer long
Whatever is begotten, born and dies.
Caught in that sensual music all neglect
Monuments of unageing intellect.

An aged man is but a paltry thing,
A tattered coat upon a stick, unless
Soul clap its hands and sing, and louder sing
For every tatter in its mortal dress,
Nor is there singing school but studying
Monuments of its own magnificence;
And therefore I have sailed the seas and come
To the holy city of Byzantium...

Once out of nature I shall never take
My bodily form from any natural thing,
But such a form as Grecian goldsmiths make
Of hammered gold and gold enamelling
To keep a drowsy Emperor awake;
Or set upon a golden bough to sing
To lords and ladies of Byzantium
Of what is past, or passing, or to come.

———————

In the last phase of his career Yeats moved towards a more private lyricism that explored contradictions and reconciliations in the physical and spiritual worlds. He was still developing the range and power of his poetry and drama when he died in 1939 in the south of France. He was buried there, and only after the end of World War II was his coffin re-interred at Drumcliff in County Sligo, in 1948.

J. M. Synge

The Irish literary renaissance was led initially by the romantic, sensuous poetry of Yeats, and the realistic prose writing of George Russell and George Moore (see page 38). However, by the turn of the century an important new voice was added, that of John Millington Synge. In 1896, Yeats had visited the Aran islands in Galway Bay off the west coast of Ireland, and meeting Synge in Paris three years later, advised him to get away from the Continent and live among the Irish peasants in order to acquire a real sense of Irish national identity. This Synge did, writing plays such as the tragedy *Riders to the Sea* (1904) and the black comedy *The Playboy of the Western World* (1907).

Both plays are set on the Aran Islands and capture the rhythm and idiom of Irish rustic speech. *The Playboy of the Western World* takes as its central character a man, Christy Mahon, who believes he has killed his father in a fight and runs away to the remote village in which the play is set. He is fêted for his deed, but when Christy's father turns up looking for his son, and Christy again tries unsuccessfully to kill him, the villagers are horrified at the idea of the murder they had only recently been celebrating. The first performances of *The Playboy of the Western World* provoked riots at the Abbey Theatre in Dublin, because the audience were disgusted at the idea that the Irish could approve of murder, not recognising that the play is really about the creation of myths, and that the rights or wrongs of murder itself are not the focus of the play's dramatic attention. Synge found a new naturalism for his work, yet drew as heavily as Yeats on the mysticism of Ireland and the Irish poetic tradition that celebrates unspoiled Nature and Man's relationship with it.

Irish fiction

At the turn of the century, drama and poetry were the dominant forms in the Irish literary revival. The main novelists at the close of the 19th century were Violet Martin (1862-1915), who wrote as Martin Ross, and Edith Somerville (1858-1949). These two upper-class cousins wrote about their own Anglo-Irish world and the Gaelic-speaking peasantry in a perceptively satirical way in *The Real Charlotte* (1894) and in a series of short stories under the titles *Some Experiences of an Irish R.M.* (1899) and *Further Experiences*

of an Irish R.M. (1908) – R.M. stands for 'resident magistrate'.
The transition to a new kind of fiction was marked by the work of
George Moore. Born in Ireland, he spent most of the first 50 years
of his life in England and France, where he was strongly influenced
by the French poet Charles Baudelaire (1821-67) and the
naturalistic French novelist Émile Zola (1840-1902). His most
successful book, *Esther Waters* (1894), was one of the first novels
in English to adopt Zola's realistic techniques.

In 1901 Moore moved to Dublin, where he enthusiastically
joined the literary revival. He was closely involved in the planning of
the Abbey Theatre, and his collection of short stories, *The Untilled
Field* (1903), was the first piece of prose in the modern, naturalistic
mode of Irish writing. His greatest contribution to Irish writing was
probably *Hail and Farewell* (1911-14), a memoir of his involvement
in the literary scene which includes portraits of Lady Gregory,
George Russell and Yeats. However, Yeats was so angry with
Moore's representation of him and his friends that he brought out
his own autobiography, *Reveries over Childhood and Youth* (1914),
to set the record straight and to offer a lyrical and intense picture of
his growth and development as a poet. Moore returned to London
in 1911, disgusted at the narrow-mindedness and pettiness of Irish
politics and society, and at the grip of the Catholic Church over the
hearts and minds of the people.

Many of the other prominent prose writers of the '20s and
'30s in Ireland are remembered as much for their skill in the art of
the short story as for their novels. Some, such as Liam O'Flaherty
(1897-1984) or Flann O'Brien (1911-66; the pen name of Brian
O'Nolan) are less widely read today. O'Flaherty is perhaps best
known for his novel *The Informer*. Flann O'Brien's finest novel is
probably *At Swim-Two-Birds* (1939), which has a highly
unconventional structure and a non-linear narrative path. Frank
O'Connor (1903-66) is still known for 'My Oedipus Complex' and
other stories, while Sean O'Faolain's (1900-91) naturalistic stories
dealing with contemporary Ireland of the '20s and '30s are a
valuable literary record of the period.

Sean O'Casey (1880-1964) was perhaps the pre-eminent
playwright writing in the immediate aftermath of the War of
Independence. A committed socialist who was initially supportive
of the nationalist movement, he took no part in the Easter Rising.
In his greatest tragicomedies *The Shadow of a Gunman* (1923),
Juno and the Paycock (1924) and *The Plough and the Stars* (1926)
he depicted the slums of Dublin and the grim struggle to survive
violence and politics through the rebellion and the civil war.

Another playwright, whose work belongs chiefly in the second
half of the century, but who began his craft in this period, is Samuel
Beckett (1906-1989). He studied French and Italian at Trinity

College, Dublin, and subsequently lived in Paris, helping Joyce to draft *Finnegans Wake* (see page 40) and experimenting with his own writing. He wrote two novels in the 1930s, moving between Ireland and France without a steady source of income. When the Germans occupied Paris he and his wife joined the Resistance movement, only narrowly escaping capture and fleeing to the south of France for the rest of the war. In 1948-9 he wrote *Waiting for Godot*, and its production in Paris in January 1953 brought him his first real public success.

James Joyce

Like many other Irish writers, James Joyce, arguably Ireland's greatest novelist, chose voluntary exile. But despite the fact that his major works were published while Joyce was living abroad, they are all firmly located in Dublin, and often give a better sense of being written 'from the inside' of Dublin life than much fiction by resident Irish writers.

Born in 1882 to a well-to-do but increasingly impoverished family, Joyce was educated at Jesuit schools, with a brief period at a Christian Brothers school. He went on to University College, Dublin, to study languages; he was strongly influenced by the work of Ibsen (see box) and the success of a review he wrote of a production of Ibsen's *When We Dead Awaken* (1899) convinced Joyce that he should become a writer. After a period of unsuccessfully trying to make a living in Dublin, and starting on a long novel based on his own childhood and adolescence, *Stephen Hero*, he met and fell in love with Nora Barnacle. They left Ireland together in October 1904 and after a spell in Pola (now in Yugoslavia), settled in Trieste (then part of Austria, now in Italy). It was there that their two children were born. Joyce worked for the Berlitz school teaching English, at the same time completing his collection of short stories, *Dubliners*, and re-writing *Stephen Hero* as *A Portrait of the Artist as a Young Man*.

— IBSEN AND SOCIAL — REALIST DRAMA

Henrik Ibsen was the great Norwegian playwright of the 19th century, who had a considerable impact on many of the progressive British writers of the early 20th century. His greatest plays, including A Doll's House *(1879),* Ghosts *(1881),* An Enemy of the People *(1882),* The Wild Duck *(1884) and* Hedda Gabler *(1890) tackled social and moral issues such as fraud, contamination and hypocrisy that contemporary Scandinavian audiences found deeply shocking.* Ghosts *(whose subject is congenital syphilis) was described by the* Daily Telegraph *as 'an open drain; a loathsome sore unbandaged; a dirty act done publicly; a lazar house with all its doors and windows open.'*

Ibsen set his plays in unremarkable middle-class homes, with ordinary characters and little excitement in terms of plot. But the naturalism and perceptiveness of his dramatic style caught the attention of progressive theatres across Europe, and from the early 1880s Ibsen's reputation as either hero or hate figure was established. The Pillars of Society (1877) was the first of Ibsen's plays to be performed in England, in 1880; the first performances of A Doll's House *nearly ten years later caused consternation among English audiences. George Bernard Shaw was quick to champion Ibsen's cause, giving a lecture on 'The Quintessence of Ibsenism' in 1890 and imitating Ibsen's use of challenging themes and bourgeois settings in his own plays such as* Mrs Warren's Profession *(1902) or* Major Barbara *(1905). The influence of the Ibsenesque social 'problem play' can also be seen in the work of Galsworthy and Harley Granville-Barker (see page 16).*

The Joyce family lived in Trieste until 1915 when they moved to Zurich in Switzerland. Meantime, Joyce had met Harriet Shaw Weaver, the editor of The Egoist magazine, who so admired his work that she provided financial support for years, and arranged for the first edition of A Portrait of the Artist as a Young Man in 1916, when once again Joyce could not persuade any publisher to accept his manuscript.

In Zurich Joyce continued to work on Ulysses, which he had started in 1914, and episodes from the unfinished novel were published by an American journal, the Little Review, until publication was banned in 1920, as the authorities were concerned at the explicit content of the writing. In that year, at the suggestion of Ezra Pound, the Joyces moved to Paris and Joyce put his energies into the publication of Ulysses. He had chosen the French capital as a place more receptive to the unconventional style and content of his novel – no publisher in Britain or the United States would touch it for fear of the legal consequences. It was finally published by Sylvia Beach, the proprietor of a well-known Paris bookshop 'Shakespeare & Co.', on Joyce's birthday, 2 February 1922.

The book immediately became a cause célèbre, and Joyce revelled in the critical praise. However, his eyesight had been poor for some time, and the mental health of his daughter, Lucia, was also a great worry. He continued to work on his final novel, Finnegans Wake, which was published in complete form in May 1939. Described as 'the great unread masterpiece of 20th-century literature' and 'the most audacious fiction in the English language', it was too impenetrable for many critics, and Joyce was disappointed by the book's reception. He died in Zurich in 1941.

— FLIGHT AND MOTION—

Joyce's works commonly take as their theme the idea of a progression or a journey from a state of ignorance and frustration to one of discovery and freedom. The short stories in Dubliners *are particularly concerned with paralysis of one kind or another. In a letter to the publisher Grant Richards, Joyce wrote: 'My intention was to write a chapter of the moral history of my country and I chose Dublin for the scene because that city seemed to me the centre of paralysis.' The characters in the stories long for various kinds of escape from the condition of their lives, but cannot achieve them.*

In A Portrait of the Artist as a Young Man, *Joyce recreates himself as Stephen Dedalus (playing on the myth of Daedalus and Icarus, see page 44) and charts his childhood and education up to his leaving Dublin for the Continent. At various points in the novel, Stephen finds a kind of release from his immediate anxieties and at the end of the novel he feels that he will be starting afresh, having fulfilled his destiny as a writer. Earlier on, walking along the mouth of the River Liffey he has a vision of his role:*

he seemed to hear the noise of dim waves and to see a winged form flying above the waves and slowly climbing the air. What did it mean? Was it a quaint device opening the page of some medieval book of prophecies and symbols, a hawk-like man flying sunward above the sea, a prophecy of the end he had been born to serve and had been following through the mists of childhood and boyhood, a symbol of the artist forging anew in his workshop out of the sluggish matter of the earth a new soaring impalpable imperishable being?

The action of Ulysses *takes place in a single day, 16 June, and follows Stephen Dedalus and his companion Leopold Bloom in their wanderings around Dublin, echoing and reworking the wanderings of the mythological hero Ulysses in his return from the Trojan wars. The scope of the book is vast; the 'stream-of-consciousness' (see Glossary of Terms) writing that Joyce uses in the book replicates the unstructured thoughts and feelings of the characters. At the end, Bloom returns home to his wife Molly (based on Joyce's wife Nora, who corresponds to Penelope, the long suffering wife of Ulysses). The last chapter records Molly's thoughts as she lies in bed in eight long paragraphs taking up nearly 80 pages.*

James Joyce, 1924

Joyce was afflicted by a succession of problems with his eyesight. From 1917 onwards he suffered from iritis, glaucoma and cataracts. He remained remarkably resilient to the pain and anxiety which these diseases and repeated operations (27 in all) caused him.

Constantin Brancusi, Sketch of James Joyce (1929)

In 1929, Joyce was in the process of writing *Finnegans Wake*, then called *Work in Progress*. The abstract sculptor Constantin Brancusi was commissioned to draw a portrait of Joyce for a book publicising the forthcoming work, and this is one of several sketches that Brancusi made of the author (below). At the same time Brancusi made a highly abstract sketch of Joyce, entitled a 'Symbol of Joyce', which was no more than a spiral and three vertical lines. This was shown to Joyce's father, who remarked: 'The boy seems to have changed a good deal.'

4. MODERNISM

Definitions

The year 1922 is an important one in the history of English
literature, as it was the year in which both James Joyce's *Ulysses*
(see page 44) and T.S. Eliot's *The Waste Land* (see page 56) were
published. With hindsight, these two authors have been seen by
critics as being at the forefront of a literary movement that was to
have a major influence on the rest of the 20th century, and which
was given the name 'Modernism'. As with many other such
'movements' the artists involved were not working within a set of
agreed principles or necessarily even aware that their work was
bracketed with that of others to form an identifiable set of shared
values or practices.

The term 'Modernism' was originally used to distinguish the
work of various artists – not just writers – whose work broke
deliberately from the traditions of the 19th century and
experimented with new ways of interpreting the world through their
art. The period from 1910 to 1930 is usually taken to be the time
during which the main artists produced their greatest work, although
the seeds of Modernism can be seen in writing from the 19th
century (Matthew Arnold's 'Dover Beach', the dramatic monologues
of Robert Browning, or the novels of Charles Dickens, for example).
The influence of Modernism continued beyond World War II, to be
subsumed into the Postmodernist movement (see Glossary of
Terms). Perhaps the essential quality of Modernism was the need to
question the consensus and to redefine things that were taken for
granted. The effect of World War I cannot be underestimated as
a reason for this questioning, since those who survived the war
were only too aware that the cost in human life, resources and
international self-confidence had been repaid by little, if any, benefit
for anyone in Europe. The values of the international community
that had led to the war, and the assumption that civilisation could
be maintained by the tacit agreement of the main European powers
had all been called into question.

Reassessing the past and the self

The chief authors associated with the Modernist movement in
Britain were T.S. Eliot, James Joyce, D.H. Lawrence, Ezra Pound and
Virginia Woolf. They came from very different cultural backgrounds,
but directly or indirectly they were all influenced by the work of
various German and Austrian thinkers from the second half of the
19th century. Karl Marx's *Communist Manifesto* (1848) and the
unfinished *Das Kapital* (*Capital*; 1867) were a wide-ranging attack
on the existing cultural, political and economic systems in Europe

and America, while the philosophical writing of Friedrich Nietzsche (1844-1900) challenged people's assumptions about religion (one of his most famous utterances was 'God is dead'), art and Western civilisation in books such as *Also Sprach Zarathustra* (*Thus Spake Zarathustra;* 1883-5).

The founder of psychoanalysis (see Glossary of Terms), Sigmund Freud, started his researches into the links between the brain and various mental conditions such as hysteria in Vienna in the 1880s. By the 1890s he had become interested in the impact of suppressed sexual feelings on mental disorder, which led in turn to investigations into the relationships between dreams and the fulfilment of fantasies and suppressed desire. His most influential work *Die Traumdeutung* (*The Interpretation of Dreams)* was published in 1900 and translated into English in 1913. It initiated a massive change in the perception of human behaviour, in particular providing a scientific basis for the idea that people are not fully in control of their emotions and feelings. A number of the novels of Henry James – *The Turn of the Screw* (1898), for example – or those of Joseph Conrad (*Heart of Darkness)* rely on an understanding of psychology to explain the behaviour and motivation of characters, and many Modernist writers showed a preoccupation with the workings of the mind and the link between sexuality and behaviour that betray Freud's influence.

A growing awareness of anthropology (the study of different civilisations and the development of human behaviour) was linked to Freud's work on psychoanalysis. The chief work of the British scholar and anthropologist Sir James Frazer (1854-1941) – *The Golden Bough* (1890 and enlarged to 12 volumes 1911-15) – examined the links between magic and religion, and drew close parallels between Christian myths and the fertility cults of the Mediterranean in pre-Roman times. T.S. Eliot acknowledged his debt to Frazer's work in his poem *The Waste Land*, which urges a rediscovery of the roots of culture and civilisation in order to repair the damage done to society

— THE BLOOMSBURY GROUP—

Between about 1905 and 1935, a group of artists, writers and thinkers met frequently to discuss art and philosophy. Initially they gathered at the homes of the daughters of the critic and scholar Sir Leslie Stephen, Vanessa Bell (1879-1961) and Virginia Woolf, which were in the Bloomsbury area of London. Many of the group had been to university at Cambridge, and among the most talented were the artist Duncan Grant (1885-1978), the biographer Lytton Strachey (1880-1932), the novelists E.M. Forster (1879-1970) and David Garnett (1892-1981), the economist John Maynard Keynes (1883-1946), the art critics Roger Fry (1866-1934) and Clive Bell (1881-1964; who married Vanessa Bell, herself an artist) and Virginia Woolf's husband Leonard, who was an important member of the Fabian Society (see page 10). Virginia and Leonard Woolf set up the Hogarth Press, which published T.S. Eliot's The Waste Land *and the English edition of Freud's works, as well as Virginia Woolf's own books. In the variety of their writing, painting and publishing, the Bloomsbury Group had considerable influence on the development of culture in the early 20th century, although its members did not share a common philosophy or espouse a particular set of values. The intellectual, artistic atmosphere of the group, which also met at Garsington Manor, the home of Lady Ottoline Morrell (1873-1938; see page 61), is caught in the collection of characters living with the Ramsays in Woolf's* To the Lighthouse.

———

as a result of over-sophistication and loss of belief. The very opening of the poem draws attention to the theme of burial and regeneration that runs throughout the poem:

> April is the cruellest month, breeding
> Lilacs out the dead land, mixing
> Memory and desire, stirring
> Dull roots with spring rain.

Myth and history

Modernist writing strove to find a new way of organising itself, relying less on the formal methods of the previous century, and instead seeking a coherence derived from an internal, subjective creativity. For this reason, myth and the workings of the mind, appealing as they do to a non-literal understanding of their method, were common to many writers of the period. In an essay entitled 'What is Modern?' (1918) the poet Edwin Muir (1887-1959) wrote:

> Let no one say that it is impossible at this stage in man's history to resuscitate Myth. The past has certainly lost its mystery for us... but the future is still ours, and there, at Man's goal, our myths must be planted. And thither, indeed, has set the great literature of the last hundred years. Faust, Mephistopheles, Brand, Peer Gynt, Zarathustra – there were no greater figures in the literature of the last century – all were myths, and all forecasts of the future.

> T. S. Eliot wrote in an essay of 1923 reviewing Joyce's *Ulysses*:

> Instead of narrative method, we may now use the mythical method. It is, I seriously believe, a step towards making the modern world possible for art.

James Joyce (see page 39) drew on both Classical and Irish mythology for the thematic inspiration of all three of his novels. In *A Portrait of the Artist as a Young Man* he weaves the myth of Daedalus and Icarus into the novel in various ways. The epigraph on the title page is taken from Book VII of Ovid's *Metamorphoses*: *Et ignotas animum dimittit in artes* ('And he sets his mind to work on unknown arts'), and describes the realisation of Daedalus that he must make wings like a bird's in order to escape from Minos, King of Crete. Images of flight, of the labyrinth (which Daedalus created for Minos) and of the pride that lured Icarus to fly too close to the sun all recur throughout the novel.

Ulysses was serialised before being published in its complete form, and in the earlier version each chapter of the novel was given the title of one of the episodes in Homer's epic poem *The Odyssey*. Thus, for example, the hero Leopold Bloom attends a funeral in the 'Hades' chapter, corresponding to Ulysses's journey into the underworld, while in the chapter headed 'Cyclops', Bloom has an argument with a citizen in a bar, and narrowly escapes a brawl. In Homer, the brutish Cyclops Polyphemus has only one eye. Joyce's Cyclops is the bigoted and xenophobic citizen, whose vision is blinkered, and can see no other point of view but his own.

D.H. Lawrence

D(avid) H(erbert) Lawrence was another forward-looking writer who turned to myth to express his ideas about human relationships. His first published novel was *Sons and Lovers* (1913), in which Lawrence fictionalised his own growing-up and close relationship with his mother. In the narrative there are correspondences with the Greek myth of Oedipus, in which Oedipus tragically fulfils a prophecy that he would kill his father and marry his mother. Freud had employed the Oedipus myth in his psychoanalytical researches to illustrate early bonding patterns and the emotional affiliations of children for the parent of the opposite gender. When this was pointed out in an early review of the novel, Lawrence was appalled; his reading of Freud's work did have a strong influence on his writing, but he disagreed with Freud's conclusions in a number of areas, particularly on the nature of the unconscious and on the acquisition of sexual feelings. In *Fantasia of the Unconscious* (1922) Lawrence wrote: 'What Freud says is always partly true. And half a loaf is better than no bread. But really, there is the other half of the loaf. All is *not* sex. And a sexual motive is *not* to be attributed to all human activities. We know it, without need to argue.'

Lawrence had been brought up as a non-conformist Christian, and although he rejected Christian belief in his early twenties, religion and a sense of the religious play an important part in his work. His second novel, *The Rainbow* (1915), draws on Christian mythology, particularly the story of Noah and the flood, to paint a picture of three generations of a Nottinghamshire family and their relationship with the land and with each other. The first chapter of the novel is written in a highly ornate, almost Biblical style as it reflects on the traditions of the Brangwen family:

> In autumn the partridges whirred up, birds in flocks blew like spray across the fallow, rooks appeared on the grey, watery heavens, and flew cawing into the winter. Then the men sat by the fire in the house where the women moved about with surety and the limbs and the body of the men were impregnated with the day, cattle and earth and vegetation and the sky, the men sat by the fire and their brains were

inert, as their blood flowed heavy with the accumulation from the living day.

The women were different. On them too was the drowse of blood-intimacy, calves sucking and hens running together in droves, and young geese palpitating in the hand while the food was pushed down their throttle. But the women looked out from the heated, blind intercourse of farm-life, to the spoken world beyond. They were aware of the lips and the mind of the world and giving utterance they heard the sound in the distance, and they strained to listen.

Lawrence and his wife Frieda were keen travellers, and among other parts of the world they visited Australia and New Mexico. The novels written in response to these places – *Kangaroo* (1923) and *The Plumed Serpent* (1926) – are an interesting reflection of Lawrence's interest in the relationship between power and myth. In *The Plumed Serpent*, for instance, a charismatic leader, Don Ramón, builds a deadly cult around the expected return of the ancient Mexican gods, casting himself as a manifestation of Quetzalcoatl, the Aztec god which is half bird, half serpent, and his co-leader Don Cipriano as Huitzilopochtli, god of the Sun.

Virginia Woolf

In her major novels Virginia Woolf made little use of shared cultural reference points, such as myth or the literature of the past, in the way that either Joyce or Lawrence did. Instead, she created internal landscapes of the mind, and examined the interplay of characters' personal perceptions of the world. Nevertheless, in this very individual world, memory, history and the passing of time played an important part. Woolf wrote *To the Lighthouse* (1927) as a conscious memorial to her parents, and the narrative of the novel is structured around the interaction of the past and the present. The expected trip by the Ramsay family to the lighthouse off the coast of Scotland never happens, and in the central section of the novel, 'Time Passes', the passage of time removes several of the family through war, childbirth and old age. The deaths of the family members are almost incidental, presented in square brackets within a description of the Ramsays' deserted and decaying house:

[Mr Ramsay stumbling along a passage stretched his arms out one dark morning, but, Mrs Ramsay having died rather suddenly the night before, he stretched his arms out. They remained empty]...

[A shell exploded. Twenty or thirty young men were blown up in France, among them Andrew Ramsay, whose death, mercifully, was instantaneous.]

Symbols, such as the stocking that Mrs Ramsay never finishes knitting throughout the first half of *To the Lighthouse*, are a feature of Woolf 's writing that is central to the Modernist method. In *Mrs Dalloway* (1925), the action of the novel takes place on a single day (as does the action in Joyce's *Ulysses*), and much of the writing reaches back into the memories of the two main characters Clarissa Dalloway and Septimus Warren Smith. The memory of World War I is strong, as Septimus is mentally disturbed as a result of his experiences in the war and the death of his best friend, Evans. The lives of both characters intersect in an unexpected way at the end of the novel, but in various symbolic ways (for instance through images of windows and movement up and down) they are seen to have more in common than meets the eye.

Modernist art

Modernism is a term applied not only to literature but to the other art forms of the 20th century. By the end of the 19th century, artists started to experiment with non-literal representations of the world around them. Impressionist painters such as Paul Gauguin (1848-1903) and Vincent Van Gogh (1853-90) had begun to move beyond the literal, having become dissatisfied with the rules and expectations of the contemporary art world, but their work was not in any sense abstract. The first artists to break firmly with the past in this respect are known as Expressionists, although the term covers a range of artists in several countries who did not subscribe to a particular manifesto, as many of the Modernist art movements did. Edvard Munch's (1863-1944) lithograph *The Cry* (1893) is an early example of the intention to communicate an emotion through every aspect of a picture, subordinating realism to the expression of feeling. One of the earliest artists to experiment with purely abstract, or non-figurative art was Wassily Kandinsky (1866-1944). He was interested in the intrinsic qualities of different colours that allow the artist to communicate to his public without the need for recognisable forms; once the subject of a painting was no longer a sacrosanct ingredient, then it was a relatively small step to remove the idea of the subject altogether. Kandinsky's explanation of his objective can apply equally to any number of other Modernist artists:

> The spectator is too ready to look for a 'meaning' in a picture… Our materialistic age has produced a type of spectator who is not content to place himself in front of a picture and let it speak for itself. Instead of letting the intrinsic values of the picture work upon him, he worries himself into looking for "closeness to nature", "temperament", "perspective" and so on. His eye does not probe the outer expression to arrive at the inner meaning.

Kandinsky arrived at his theory of abstract art over a period of time, having been influenced by the later stages of the Impressionist movement and in particular Fauvism, which literally means beast-ism, and was so-called because of the vibrant colours and warped forms of its exponents' paintings. The leading artist of the Fauvist group was Henri Matisse (1869-1954), who felt that the strength of plain colours and the spontaneity of the image was a natural response to his emotions towards his subject. Fauvism lasted from 1905 for only a few years, and was succeeded from 1907 onwards by one of the most influential theories of 20th century art – Cubism.

Cubism and after

From 1907, both Pablo Picasso and Georges Braque (1882-1963) began to experiment with new ways of representing a subject on a two-dimensional plane – the artist's canvas. They did this by doing away with the idea of perspective, painting objects from multiple viewpoints and dismembering objects so that different aspects of the form are accentuated and realigned to present them as they appear in the mind rather than to the eye. Picasso's first Cubist painting, Les Demoiselles d'Avignon (1907), caused critical consternation when it was first shown, because it broke many of the 'rules' about the representation of the human form and the composition of a painting. The art of Picasso, Braque and others such as Jean Metzinger (1883-1956) and Albert Gleizes (1881-1953) developed towards the use of collage, using objects such as newspapers to represent themselves as well as being a part of the overall composition. In a manner not dissimilar from the writers of the period, these two artists and the other Cubists were concerned less with the subject of their art than with the ways in which they could communicate reality through form.

One distinct movement that owed much to Cubism was originated by the Italian poet Filippo Marinetti. In 1909 he published his so-called 'Futurist Manifesto'. This was an all-embracing proposal for the regeneration of Italian art and culture, which Marinetti saw as decadent and stagnant. Futurism glorified the strength of the machine, the totality of war, the ecstasy of speed and the aggressive advance of the industrial present. Artists such as Gino Severini (1883-1966), Umberto Boccioni (1882-1916) and Giacomo Balla (1871-1958) employed the principles of Cubism to communicate the effect of 'dynamism' (a key Futurist expression) and speed: the geometric arrangement of the elements of a painting break up the physical form of its subject and so communicate a sense of its movement rather than its entity. The fascination for Futurist artists of the machine and the conflict of dynamic forces suffered a fatal blow when World War I broke out, as

Imperial Airways Handley Page HP 42 class aeroplane at Croydon Airport

The Handley Page HP 42 or 'Heracles' class of aeroplane was the first four-engined aircraft in the world. It was designed to fly on new European routes developed by Imperial Airways in the late 1920s and '30s and also intercontinental routes to Egypt, the Arabian Gulf, India, South Africa, Singapore and West Africa. A route to Australia was opened in 1935. The HP 42 seated either 24 or 38 passengers, according to its destination, and it was the only airliner of the time to provide a full catering service, of a four- or seven-course meal. Imperial Airways flew from Croydon Airport in south London, then a major international terminus.

so many lives were wasted as a result of the first mechanised conflict, and the movement did not survive the war.

A movement with close links to the Futurists was led by Percy Wyndham Lewis. Lewis collaborated with Ezra Pound in the publication of two issues of a new journal entitled *Blast: The Review of the Great English Vortex* in July 1914 and 1915. *Blast*, like Marinetti's 'Futurist Manifesto', attacked the reactionary tendencies of British cultural life, typified by the Bloomsbury group (see box on page 43), and advocated total acceptance of the machine age, and a mechanical, geometrical and non-representational approach to art in imitation of Cubism and Futurism. The new movement was known as Vorticism, and attracted other artists such as the sculptor Henri Gaudier-Brzeska (1891-1915) and C.R.W. Nevinson (see page 25). Among the authors who contributed articles to the two editions of *Blast* were T.S. Eliot, Ford Madox Ford (1873-1939) and Rebecca West (1892-1983). Lewis enlisted in the Royal Artillery and served at the front before being appointed an official war artist (see illustration on page 51).

Surrealism

If Vorticism and Futurism took as their starting point a highly authoritarian and prescriptive set of principles, another of the most influential Modernist movements, Surrealism, could be said to be largely anarchic in its objectives. It emerged as a development of Dada, an anti-war protest movement which lasted from 1915 to the early 1920s. Dadaism reacted against the very idea of art itself through various anti-aesthetic creations. Its chief figures included the artists Jean Arp (1887-1966) and Marcel Duchamp (1887-1968), and the poet Tristan Tzara (1896-1963) who shocked and insulted their public by producing works such as a urinal on a stand, or scraps of coloured paper torn up at random and then stuck on to the floor as an expression of the artist's lack of control over his art.

— *BLAST* —

Blast was designed in a highly aggressive written style with a bold typeface and other typographical features to push home the attack on old-fashioned values that the Vorticist movement pursued. The following extract is taken from the first issue, published in 1914:

'*To make the rich of the community shed their education skin, to destroy politeness, standardization and academic, that is civilised, vision, is the task we have set ourselves.*

We want to make in England not a popular art, not a revival of lost folk art, or a romantic fostering of such unactual conditions, but to make individuals, wherever found.

We will convert the King if possible.

A VORTICIST KING! WHY NOT?

DO YOU THINK LLOYD GEORGE HAS THE VORTEX IN HIM?

AUTOMOBILISM (Marinetteism) bores us. We don't want to go about making a hulla-bulloo about motor cars, anymore than about knives and forks, elephants or gas-pipes.

Elephants are VERY BIG. Motor cars go quickly.'

———————

Percy Wyndham Lewis,
A Battery Shelled **(1919)**

Wyndham Lewis served in an artillery battery and saw action for six
months in the Ypres Salient in 1917. He was employed by both the
British and the Canadians as an official war artist (see page 50)
and *A Battery Shelled* was a commission by the British Ministry of
Information, which he started in April 1919. Lewis's Vorticist techniques
can be seen in the emphatic use of line and geometry, and there is a
strong tension between the activity in the battery and in the air, and the
calm detachment of the three spectators on the right of the picture.

The poet André Breton (1896-1966) published the 'Surrealist Manifesto' in Paris in 1924. Like Dada, this new movement negated the rational and the formal, but whereas Dada reduced everything to a state of meaninglessness, Surrealism was a more positive movement, influenced by Freud's ideas on the workings of the subconscious and the influence of sex and death on the human psyche. The lack of regard for a literal representation of a subject, putting in its place a symbolic, dream-like world in which apparently unconnected forms and concepts emerge from one another, offered an unstructured approach to the objective of representing what the mind sees rather than the eye. In this regard, it was like Cubism, but Cubism differed from Surrealism in being highly formal. Surrealism began as a literary movement: Breton worked with other poets including Paul Éluard (1895-1952) and Pierre Reverdy (1889-1960) to produce writing that took as its starting point a psychological rather than logical approach to its construction. However, it is the movement's art that became most well known through the work of Max Ernst (1891-1976), Joan Miró (1893-1983), René Magritte (1898-1967) and Salvador Dali (1904-89).

Imagism

Throughout the Modernist period there was a close association between the visual arts and literature – poetry in particular. For example, the poet Ezra Pound was a founding member of the Vorticist movement, and André Breton of the Surrealist movement. Pound had a restless intellect, and his first foray into creating a literary grouping was the establishment of the 'Imagist' school in about 1912. This was a group of American and English writers who were inspired by the thinking of the critic and anti-romantic philosopher T.E. Hulme (1883-1917). The Imagists sought to abandon the conventions of the 19th century, such as literary formality and the use of regular rhyme and rhythm in poetry, by focusing entirely on creating images in their writing that were clear and concentrated. In order to keep the focus on the image, the poet was not bound by the usual requirements of rhythm or subject matter, and the writing was condensed and unromantic.

Pound and his fellow Imagists were following in the footsteps of a group of French poets at the end of the 19th century (chiefly Stéphane Mallarmé, Charles Baudelaire, Paul Verlaine and Arthur Rimbaud) known as the Symbolists whose aim was to evoke personal mood and feeling indirectly through reference to colour, sound and sense. In the same way that there was a close affinity between Symbolist poetry and music, Imagist poetry sought to find similarities with sculpture in its lack of superfluous decoration and the clarity of its lines. Another strong influence was the Japanese *haiku*, a short poem that captures a single facet of nature in exactly

17 syllables. Besides Pound, the movement included the American poets Hilda Doolittle (see page 29), William Carlos Williams (1883-1963) and Amy Lowell (1874-1925); the critic and novelist Richard Aldington (see page 29) and D.H. Lawrence (see page 45). When Pound moved on to embrace Vorticism, Lowell took over leadership of the group, which Pound dismissively chose to call 'Amygism'. Perhaps the most familiar example of Imagist verse is Pound's two line poem, 'In a Station of the Metro':

> The apparition of these faces in the crowd,
> Petals on a wet, black bough.

In this poem there is a metaphorical connection between the two lines, which deepens the reader's understanding of the image. In Richard Aldington's 'Evening', there is only the image itself:

> The chimneys, rank on rank,
> Cut the clear sky;
> The moon,
> With a rig of gauze about her loins
> Poses among them, an awkward Venus –
> And here am I looking wantonly at her
> Over the kitchen sink.

Although Imagism lasted a relatively short time – it was too prescriptive to endure for long – it was to prove highly influential on poets such as W.B. Yeats and T.S. Eliot, and so on the direction of 20th-century poetry as a whole.

Music

Riots accompanied the first performances of Synge's *The Playboy of the Western World* at the Abbey Theatre in 1907 (see page 37), and a similar fate befell the opening night of a new ballet by the Russian composer Igor Stravinsky (1882-1971) in Paris in May 1913. The ballet was *The Rite of Spring*, and the occasion established Stravinsky as the leading Modernist composer of the day. Stravinsky had already made a reputation through his collaboration with the great Russian impresario Serge Diaghilev (1872-1929) to write the ballets *The Firebird* (1910) and *Petrushka* (1911). While finishing the score for *The Firebird*, Stravinsky had 'a fleeting vision… I saw in my imagination a solemn pagan rite: sage elders, seated in a circle, watched a young girl dance herself to death. They were sacrificing her to propitiate [satisfy] the god of spring.' The music that he wrote to put this vision into sound was *The Rite of Spring*. It was barbaric and violent in its emphasis on relentless, uneven rhythms and unchanging dissonant harmony, and as soon as the first performance began, shouts of protest were heard, followed by increasingly violent reactions among the audience.

In one sense, Stravinsky was representing musically the same instincts that Sir James Frazer had identified in *The Golden Bough* (see page 43), or that Yeats communicated through his poetry (see page 35). *The Rite of Spring* was still provoking strong reactions in 1921, when T.S. Eliot attended a performance at Covent Garden in London. He was so infuriated with the laughter of the audience that he poked his neighbours with the point of his umbrella to make them shut up. He thought that the music transformed 'the rhythm of the steppes into the scream of the motor-horn, the rattle of machinery, the grind of wheels, the beating of iron and steel, the roar of the underground railway, and the other barbaric noises of modern life.' Stravinsky's subsequent musical style became much more restrained as he was drawn to a Neoclassical idiom, and only towards the end of his career was he moved to experiment with the other great Modernist movement, serialism.

Atonality and serialism

The composer Arnold Schoenberg (1874-1951) grew up in a culture of amateur music-making in Vienna, teaching himself theory and writing pieces for the groups of friends with whom he played. The early influences on his style were the German opera composer Richard Wagner (1813-83) and Johannes Brahms (1833-97). In his thirties Schoenberg took up painting, exhibiting his paintings in Vienna in 1910. In the same way that Kandinsky (who was a friend of Schoenberg) and the Expressionists looked for ways to express abstract ideas and a more subjective interpretation of experience that representational art could not satisfy (see page 47), Schoenberg

— EZRA POUND AND THE— ENGLISH LITERARY SCENE

Born in Idaho, Ezra Pound attended the University of Pennsylvania, where he met his long-standing friend, the poet William Carlos Williams. In 1908 he left America for London, where he became friends with James Joyce, Wyndham Lewis and the editor of the influential journal, The English Review, Ford Madox Ford. He published several collections of poems between 1909 and 1914, and his collaboration with the sculptor Henri Gaudier-Brzeska and Wyndham Lewis led to the founding of the Vorticist movement and the publication of Blast (see page 50). He worked hard on Joyce's behalf to secure the publication of both A Portrait of the Artist as a Young Man and Ulysses, advising Joyce at every stage of the writing of Ulysses and finding sources of income for his impoverished friend. Pound published some of T.S. Eliot's earliest poetry in The Egoist and when Pound moved in 1921 to Paris, he worked on the manuscript of Eliot's next undertaking, The Waste Land. He halved the poem, reducing the narrative elements and making it more in keeping with the Modernist times.

At the same time that he was working with other authors, Pound continued to write his own poetry. Many of his best Imagist poems were collected in Lustra (1916), while Hugh Selwyn Mauberley (1920) is probably his finest work, a reflection of his profound disillusionment with British life and culture in the period either side of World War I. He had played a pivotal role in the forging of a modern literary culture in England by the time he moved to Italy in 1924. He stayed in Italy for 20 years, becoming involved in the rise of Fascism under Mussolini (see page 68). During World War II he became actively anti-American, broadcasting regularly on behalf of the Italian authorities from Rome against the American war effort. He was arrested and imprisoned for six months, then transferred to the United States. There he was charged with treason, but was declared mentally unfit to stand trial and so confined to a mental hospital for the 'criminally insane' in Washington D.C. Released in 1958, when the charges against him were dropped, he returned to Italy, where he wrote no more until his death in 1972. His ongoing poem The Cantos was begun in 1915, sections of which were published throughout his writing career, but it remained unfinished at his death.

sought after a musical technique that went beyond the conventional 'language' of 19th-century composition. His first major composition, *Verklärte Nacht* ('Transfigured Night'; 1899) was tonally conventional, but combined different elements of orchestral and chamber music, which appalled the musical establishment. In the first decade of the 20th century he wrote music that moved further and further away from 'tonality' (music is tonal when it is written in a set of related keys that correspond harmonically to one another). In 1909, Schoenberg wrote 'Three Pieces for Piano', Op. 11, which has the distinction of being the first atonal composition. He pursued this new direction in subsequent works, despite violent criticism from the musical establishment, and found support in two of his pupils, Anton Webern (1883-1945) and Alban Berg (1885-1935). The three composers collectively became known as the Second Viennese School.

After World War I, Schoenberg, Webern and Berg continued to advance the cause of new music. In the early 1920s, Schoenberg adopted a yet more radical compositional method, known as the 'twelve-tone technique', about which he declared to a pupil in 1921: 'Today I have discovered something which will assure the supremacy of German music for the next 100 years.' The twelve-tone method, also known as serial music, is based on a sequence of 12 notes, which the composer is able to manipulate in various ways in the course of the composition. In the course of time, this approach to composition became more accepted, and by the time of his death in 1951, Schoenberg was widely respected, particularly in the United States, where he settled after being victimised by the Nazis (his parents were both Jewish) in 1933.

Fragmentation and dissolution

Much of the art and literature described in this chapter is based on the rejection of 19th-century traditions and the consensus between the artist and his or her public. Modernist artists, writers and musicians found new means of using the language or form of their own particular art form to achieve a new level of abstraction that the narrative or representational conventions of the 19th century had not permitted. In particular, many Modernists used fragmentation as an expression of experience. The work of Picasso or Kandinsky, the atonal music of Schoenberg, or the writing of Joyce, Eliot or Woolf, explore their subject from multiple viewpoints in a non-literal, non-chronological manner and in so doing expose aspects of human experience – obscenity and mental disorder in particular – that had long been kept out of the public view in art.

Although many Modernists protested that their work was not 'difficult', it presented (and still presents) challenges to its audience that earlier art did not. It required the viewer, listener or reader to establish meaning or coherence from a form that was fragmentary, requiring greater effort of understanding and a degree of creativity. In many cases, it was also highly allusive, referring to other works of art or parts of the cultural heritage, which led some critics to accuse it of being elitist because it spoke only to an audience that understood such references. It was also accused of being overly self-conscious, drawing attention to its artificiality and its difference from the art of the past. The closing lines of Eliot's *The Waste Land*, in which all the themes and symbols of the poem are drawn together in a final collage of sounds and images, epitomise many of the qualities of Modernist writing:

> I sat upon the shore
> Fishing, with the arid plain behind me
> Shall I at least set my lands in order?
> London Bridge is falling down falling
> down falling down
> *Poi s'ascose nel foco che gli affina*
> *Quando fiam uti chelidon* – O swallow
> swallow
> *Le Prince d'Aquitaine à la tour abolie*
> These fragements I have shored against
> my ruins
> Why then Ile fit you. Hieronymo's mad
> againe.
> Datta. Dayadhvam. Damyata.
> Shantih shantih shantih

— **ARCHITECTURE** —

The machine age, which brought with it new building materials, changes in working and living habits, and new perspectives on the functions of buildings, saw innovations in architecture no less dramatic than in the other arts. The chief developments were in Germany and the USA, not least because those two countries had overtaken the rest of Europe at the forefront of industrial progress. The first skyscrapers were built in the United States in the 1880s and 90s, capitalising on the development of the passenger lift and of iron and concrete as load-bearing building materials. In Germany, various groupings of architects and designers worked on ways in which high design standards could be applied to industrial buildings and products. The architectural group Deutscher Werkbund exhibited exciting new buildings in 1914 using glass, steel and reinforced concrete within the form of largely classical designs.

One of the leading members of this group, Walter Gropius (1883-1969) went on to establish an industrial design school in 1919. In 1925 Gropius designed a new building for the school, which took its name from the school itself, the Bauhaus. The building consisted of three linked blocks, providing workshops, classrooms and residential flats for the students, and was completely radical in giving priority to the logical use of space and structure, rather than starting from the imposition of rules of symmetry or proportion, upon which all Classical and neo-Classical architecture was based. Gropius's principles in the construction of the Bauhaus — asymmetry, rectangular form, light spaces through the extensive use of glass, and the use of modern materials — were rapidly adopted by other architects, such as the Dutch 'De Stijl' group, the Swiss architect Charles-Edouard Jeanneret (1887-1965; known as Le Corbusier) and Mies van der Rohe (1886-1969). In the United States, Frank Lloyd Wright (1867-1959) took a similarly innovative approach to domestic architecture. He started from the premise that the rooms in a house were more important than its outside appearance; he linked rooms in flowing, 'organic' designs that reflected the needs of the owners, creating asymetrical and plain external façades in a way that became known as the 'Prairie style'.

5. WOMEN IN SOCIETY AND LITERATURE (1900-45)

The campaign for voting rights

The literature of the early 20th century reflected the political and social concerns of many of the writers and thinkers of the day. George Bernard Shaw used his plays to dramatise the contemporary arguments about class, war, marriage and women's rights; in their novels John Galsworthy, Arnold Bennett and E.M. Forster gave close scrutiny to the failings of the middle class and its preoccupations; H.G. Wells's novel *Ann Veronica* (1909) took a suffragette as its central character. The cause of women's rights was among the most public of all social issues. The Women's Social and Political Union (WSPU) had been founded in 1903 by Emmeline Pankhurst (1857-1928) and her daughter Christabel (1880-1958). Its objective was to gain equal voting rights for women. In 1905, Christabel and another member of the WSPU were arrested after disrupting a Liberal Party meeting, and in the following year, the word 'suffragette', referring to the term for the right to vote ('suffrage'), was coined by the *Daily Mail* in a report of a meeting between the Prime Minister and the campaigners. In 1907, 3000 women marched from Hyde Park in support of 'Votes for Women'. There was a non-militant side to the movement, the National Union of Women's Suffrage Societies, led by Millicent Fawcett (1847-1929), but it was the activists who attracted attention and raised the profile of the cause. As they met with firm resistance to their demands, the suffragettes resorted to increasingly violent and militant methods, including window-smashing and stone-throwing, chaining themselves to the railings outside Downing Street, and arson attacks on churches and empty houses.

In a leaflet published in 1912 Christabel Pankhurst put the case as follows:

> It is only simple justice that women demand. They have worked for their political enfranchisement as men never worked for it, by a constitutional agitation carried on a far greater scale than any franchise agitation in the past. For fifty years they have been striving and have met with nothing but trickery and betrayal at the hands of politicians. Cabinet Ministers have taunted them with their reluctance to use the violent methods that were being used by men before they won the extension of the franchise in 1829, in 1832 and in 1867 [the dates of Reform Acts giving the vote to certain categories of male voters]. They have used women's dislike of violence as a reason for withholding from them the rights

of citizenship... The message of the broken pane is that women are determined that the lives of their sisters shall no longer be broken, and that in future those who have to obey the law shall have a voice in saying what the law shall be. Repression cannot break the spirit of liberty.

In 1913, Emmeline Pankhurst was arrested for inciting supporters to burn down the country house of David Lloyd George, then chancellor of the exchequer, and in the same year a suffragette called Emily Davison ran on to the racecourse at the Derby wearing a WSPU banner and tried to grab the reins of the king's horse. She was trampled and died shortly afterwards.

The authorities reacted to this pressure with strong-arm tactics, but found that imprisonment alone was not a sufficient deterrent, as the campaigners immediately went on hunger strike, and in many cases attempted suicide when force fed. In 1913, the 'Cat and Mouse' Act was passed, so nicknamed because its objective was to allow hunger-striking prisoners to be freed in order that they could recover their health before being re-imprisoned without any further trial. In that year, Emmeline Pankhurst herself was imprisoned, released and rearrested no fewer than 13 times.

A temporary truce was called by both sides on the outbreak of World War I, and all those suffragettes in prison were released. In the same way that many Irishmen dropped their grievances against England on the outbreak of war (see page 30), so too the great majority of women were prepared to forget their campaign for the vote in support of the politicians' war. 'Votes for Women' was replaced with 'Your Country Needs You', and women took the place of men in almost every sphere of industrial activity, in foundries, machine-gun and shell factories and shipyards, and working as carpenters, bus drivers, policewomen, sanitary inspectors and blacksmiths. The number of women in employment rose from 22 million to 42 million, but only 'for the duration of the war'.

In 1917 the new coalition administration under Lloyd George prepared a Bill to give limited voting rights to women, and in 1918 the Representation of the People Act was passed, giving the vote to married women over 30. Women now accounted for roughly 40 per cent of the electorate, but this was little satisfaction to the campaigners. As Millicent Fawcett put it: 'An age limit of thirty was imposed upon women, not because it was in any way logical or reasonable, but simply and solely to produce a constituency in which the men were not outnumbered by the women.' Many men returning from the war had lost their rights to the rented property they had occupied before being called up, and at that time the right to vote was dependent upon ownership or qualifying occupation of property. The government was therefore anxious not

A protester being led away from a suffragette attack on Buckingham Palace, 21 May 1914
Suffragette activity, which had steadily increased since 1905, came to an end with the outbreak of war in August 1914.

to 'disadvantage' the men who had been disenfranchised in this way by the war.

After World War I

During World War I women enjoyed better health and, in many cases, better prosperity than before. Unemployment fell to minimal levels, and the combination of better wages for women, provision of food at works canteens and various welfare measures meant that they ate a better diet, and in many cases enjoyed a greater sense of self-esteem. It was during the war that many habits and social expectations about women's behaviour began to change: wearing trousers, socialising without men in pubs and restaurants, playing football, smoking in public aroused considerable hostility, but the door was open, and the younger generation felt sufficiently independent and confident not to allow it to be shut again.

D.H. Lawrence captured the spirit of the times in his short story 'Tickets, Please' (1918), in which a group of young ticket collectors on a Midlands tram service humiliate their male supervisor:

> This, the most dangerous tram-service in England, as the authorities themselves declare, with pride, is entirely conducted by girls and driven by rash men, a little crippled, or by delicate young men, who creep forward in terror. The girls are fearless young hussies. In their ugly blue uniforms, skirts up to their knees, shapeless old peaked caps on their heads, they have all the *sang-froid* of an old non-commissioned officer. With a tram packed with howling colliers, roaring hymns downstairs and a sort of antiphony of obscenities upstairs, the lasses are perfectly at their ease. They pounce on the youths who try to evade their ticket machine. They push off the men at the end of their distance. They are not going to be done in the eye – not they. They fear nobody – and everybody fears them.

However, when the men returned from service after the war and were demobilised, women were, in many cases, forced to abandon the jobs they had held so successfully, since they had only been employed 'for the duration of the war'. Where they were able to keep their employment, they were paid discriminatory wages. This blow to women's economic independence coincided with the fact that over 2 million British men had been killed or wounded in the war, leaving widows to earn their own living, or wives as the sole earner in the family in an economic climate where prices had doubled since 1914. On the one hand, the personal tragedies of thousands of families often created a sense of domestic obligation towards maimed or shell-shocked partners, requiring wives and

— PATRONAGE AND PRIVILEGE —

Women played an important role in the patronage of the arts. One notable example in France was the Princesse de Polignac, an American heiress (she was a member of the Singer family, of sewing machine fame) who married a French nobleman and became the leading promoter of avant-garde music in Paris. Many composers, including Maurice Ravel (1875-1937) and Francis Poulenc (1899-1963) benefited from her generosity in promoting their music. In Ireland, Lady Augusta Gregory (see page 35) was at the forefront of the Irish literary revival in her collaboration with Yeats and Edward Martyn, and in her role in the founding of the Abbey Theatre, Dublin. Yeats repaid Lady Gregory with a number of poetic tributes to her estate at Coole Park, such as 'Coole Park and Ballylee, 1931':

Beloved books that famous hands have bound,
Old marble heads, old pictures every where;
Great rooms where travelled men and children found
Content or joy; a last inheritor
Where none has reigned that lacked a name and fame
Or out of folly into folly came.

A spot whereon the founders lived and died
Seemed once more dear than life...

Another literary patron during this period was Lady Ottoline Morrell, who formed a circle of artists and authors that met at her country house at Garsington Manor near Oxford, where she lived with her husband, a Liberal MP. The circle included D.H. Lawrence, Virginia Woolf, the philosopher Bertrand Russell (1872-1970) and Aldous Huxley. Having quarrelled with Lady Ottoline in 1915, Lawrence presented an unflattering portrait of her as Hermione Roddice in his novel Women in Love *(1921), which sealed the end of their friendship:*

'Hermione came down to dinner strange and sepulchral, her eyes heavy and full of sepulchral darkness, strength. She had put on a dress of stiff old greenish brocade, that fitted tight and made her look tall and rather terrible, ghastly. In the gay light of the drawing-room she was uncanny and oppressive. But seated in the half light of the dining-room, sitting stiffly before the shaded candles on the table she seemed a power, a presence... She took very little part in the conversation, yet she heard it all, it was all hers.'

---

daughters to care for their menfolk; on the other, women still
wanted or needed to go out to work, even though the system was
working against them. As Irene Clephane, a female commentator
at the time, observed:

> Women, whose able fulfilment of their duties had won them
> ecstatic praise, found themselves no longer wanted in a
> changed world where all the doors that had so miraculously
> opened to them were relentlessly closing again. From being
> the saviours of the nation, women in employment were
> degraded in the public press to a position of ruthless self
> seekers depriving men and their dependents of a livelihood.

The edge had been taken off the activism of the suffragette
movement by the war, and after 1918 it broadened its objectives to
include other feminist causes. The war had proved women's ability
to contribute to the national cause at a time of crisis, and political
attitudes towards their demands had softened with the ascendancy
of the Labour Party (see page 10) and Stanley Baldwin's leadership
of the Conservative party. During the 1920s, various milestones
were passed: in 1920 women were allowed to qualify as lawyers
and accountants; in 1922 women were admitted to Oxford
University and to the Civil Service; in 1919 Nancy Astor (see page
31) became the first female MP (a total of 36 women were elected
between 1918 and 1939); in 1923 men and women were given
equal grounds for divorce by the Matrimonial Causes Act. Finally, in
1928, the age restriction on women's voting rights was lifted and all
women were given the vote on the same basis as men. Emmeline
Pankhurst, who had been selected as a Conservative MP for
Whitechapel in east London in 1926 but had been forced to stand
down owing to ill health, died only a matter of weeks after the
1928 Representation of the People Act was passed.

Women's influence in the changing social fabric was strong at
a local level. The Women's Institute movement was created in the
first decade of the century, and within a short time its members
were working for many improvements in domestic affairs, while
women's appointments as magistrates or local councillors gave
them the opportunity to make improvements and promote the
cause of sexual equality, though never at the pace at which they
would have liked. Party politics played a significant part in the
preoccupations of different feminist groupings. Women in the
Labour movement had different objectives, based on their
understanding of the needs of working-class families, from those
who belonged to the Conservative Party. Incidents such as the
General Strike of 1926, and the lock-out of miners by their
employers that followed it, drew clear divisions between the classes.

Nevertheless, at times and in certain circumstances the common cause of fighting for women's issues in a male world gave women a greater bond than party differences.

Women worked to have greater influence in world affairs as well. There were a number of international women's organisations, such as the Women's International League for Peace and Freedom, and the International Women's Co-Operative Guild which campaigned for disarmament and better education for peace. With the rise of Fascism in Europe in the 1930s (see page 68) the feminist cause became more closely associated with the pacifist movement, marching in the large demonstrations against Fascism in the east end of London. A number of women volunteered to defend the Republicans against the Fascists in the Spanish Civil War (see page 71).

Sex and sexuality

In *Brave New World* (1932) by Aldous Huxley, the writer imagines a world in which society has been stratified into different socio-economic groups, maintained through genetic controls. At the top of the hierarchy the Alphas enjoy a comfortable and privileged lifestyle, while the Epsilons at the bottom have been genetically engineered and then cloned to provide manual labour and menial service without the mental capacity to question their place or role in society. The novel is a satire on the increasing dependence of society on technology and material well-being; drugs and sex without responsibility (all children are produced by in-vitro fertilisation or IVF) are the means by which the population is kept placid, but the main characters are not happy.

Huxley's novel reflects many of the concerns of the period. Recognition of the link between fertility and economic prosperity, and gradual changes in the role of women at work and at home, led to a decline in the birth rate among the working class between the wars, and small families with just one or two children became the

—**VERA BRITTAIN (1893-1970)**—

Most of the memoirs of World War I were written by men, and so Vera Brittain wrote her autobiographical account of her life up to 1925, Testament of Youth *(1933), as a deliberate counter-balance to the male perspective of the war. Brittain was studying at Somerville College, Oxford when war broke out; she volunteered as a Voluntary Aid Detachment nurse and served in London, France and Malta for the rest of the war. Her fiancé Roland Leighton was shot by a sniper in 1915, her brother Edward died on the Italian Front in 1918, and she also lost two other close friends in the war. Her experience of being both actively involved in the war and an indirect victim of the fighting gave* Testament of Youth *a great power and intensity, and its stark commentary on the effect of war gained her an international reputation. Having started out for France with idealistic expectations, within three weeks she had changed her view completely:*

> *It was very hard to believe that not far away men were being slain ruthlessly… The destruction of men, as though beasts, whether they be English, French, German or anything else, seems a crime to the whole march of civilisation.*

After the war Brittain became increasingly involved in the women's peace movement and worked with great energy both before and during World War II to promote non-violent reconciliation. Her outspoken attacks on saturation bombing during World War II were received badly by mainstream public opinion. The sequel to Testament of Youth, *called* Testament of Friendship *(1940), recorded Brittain's close relationship with the novelist and feminist Winifred Holtby (1898-1935), with whom she lived during the '20s and early '30s.*

---

norm. Marie Stopes (1880-1958) founded the first birth control clinic in 1921, which aroused great opposition from both the Catholic and Anglican churches as well as non-religious traditionalists who saw childbearing as the natural role of women. In 1923, Stopes was accused by a Catholic clergyman of 'exposing the poor to experiment'; she sued him for libel and won the case, attracting much publicity for her cause. Other reformers in favour of birth control were motivated by the desire to reduce poverty and poor social conditions. Stopes's stimulus was more centred on the woman: reduced child bearing improved the conditions and quality of marriage, and put less physical strain on mothers.

At the same time as attitudes to sexual practices within marriage began to open up, attitudes to sex outside marriage were slow to change. The pressure on parents to marry their daughters safely, and on young women to keep their love affairs to themselves, was great. To give birth to an illegitimate child often had serious consequences. If the father refused to marry the girl, then she might well be disowned by her family, be forced into giving birth in an institution (workhouses were renamed Public Assistance Institutions in 1929), then giving up the child for adoption. In some cases, the mother would be confined indefinitely to a mental asylum under the Mental Deficiency Act of 1913. Abortion was rarely a simple alternative: although illegal (until 1967) it was widely available, but fees were high, and there was a fairly high risk of death or permanent damage to the mother's health.

The literature of the period reflects the range of reactions to the changing patterns of sexual behaviour, although the work of the more notable authors was usually liberal in its approach. D.H. Lawrence's *The Rainbow* was banned on the grounds of obscenity when first published in 1915, on account of the frank descriptions of sexual activity (innocuous by modern standards) and the implied lesbian relationship between two of the characters. *Lady Chatterley's Lover*, although started in 1926 and first published privately in 1928, was not published openly until after a famous obscenity trial in 1960.

Homosexuality and lesbianism were treated as 'deviant' in the inter-war years, but the writers of the time reflected their feelings nevertheless. Both *The Rainbow* and its sequel *Women in Love* (1921) treat lesbian and latent homosexual relationships openly. In 1928, the novelist Marguerite Radclyffe Hall (1886-1943) published a novel, *The Well of Loneliness*, about the love between two female ambulance drivers. The book was immediately prosecuted for obscenity: the trial judge was of the opinion that although the book was respectably written, it encouraged people to recognise lesbianism and not to find fault with the practice. The book was banned for 21 years, despite the support of leading literary figures such as E.M. Forster and Virginia Woolf for its availability. Radclyffe Hall enjoyed a long-standing lesbian relationship, and her short hair and masculine clothes contributed to the gradual shift from a sign of female independence to a distinctive dress style for lesbians during the period.

The most joyous treatment of gender is Virginia Woolf's novel *Orlando* (1928). Woolf described the book as a 'writer's holiday', and it tells the story of Orlando, an Elizabethan nobleman who lives through the reigns of successive monarchs, becomes ambassador to Turkey to Charles II, where he finds he has become a woman. Living on as a female aristocrat through the next two centuries, she becomes a successful author in the early years of the twentieth century. Woolf was in love with Vita Sackville-West, an aristocratic novelist and poet who lived with her husband, the diplomat Harold Nicolson, at Knole Park near Sevenoaks, Kent. The character of Orlando was modelled on Sackville-West herself, the novel is described as 'a biography' on the title page, and Woolf included in the first edition of the novel in a joking way reproductions of a number of the family portraits hanging at Knole. Woolf describes the fantasy of an unexpected sex change in a gently teasing manner:

> But let other pens treat of sex and sexuality; we quit such odious subjects as soon as we can. Orlando has now washed, and dressed herself in those Turkish coats and trousers that can be worn indifferently by either sex; and was forced to consider her position. That it was precarious and embarrassing in the extreme must be the first thought of every reader who has followed her story with sympathy. Young, noble, beautiful, she had woken to find herself in a position than which we can conceive none more delicate for a young lady of rank. We should not have blamed her had she rung the bell, screamed, or fainted. But Orlando showed no such signs of perturbation.

— DETECTIVE FICTION—

Popular fiction provided escape from the concerns and worries of the early 20th century, and although spy stories and thrillers were generally the preserve of writers such as John Buchan and Herman McNeile (known as 'Sapper'), two female novelists were unchallenged in their mastery of one particular form – the detective story.

Agatha Christie (1890-1976) remains the most success-ful of all British crime writers. Her first novel, The Mysterious Affair at Styles *was published in 1920, and introduced the character of Hercule Poirot, who featured in many of her subsequent books. Her other main character, Miss Marple, first appeared in* The Murder at the Vicarage *(1930). Christie wrote over 80 novels, and those written in the '20s and '30s repre-sent the high-water mark of detective fiction, which relies heavily on plot and dialogue, providing little in the way of character or description.*

Dorothy L. Sayers (1893-1957) enjoyed a reputation in the '40s and '50s as a playwright and translator, but she is chiefly known for her highly successful novels based on the character of Lord Peter Wimsey, starting with Whose Body *(1923) and including* The Five Red Herrings *(1931) and* The Nine Tailors *(1934), set in the Fens in East Anglia where Sayers grew up. In* Strong Poison *(1930) she introduced the character of Harriet Vane, and in the last of her detective novels,* Busman's Honeymoon *(1937), Vane and Wimsey marry.*

6. THE THIRTIES AND WORLD WAR II

The Thirties began in the shadow of major economic depression and ended under the cloud of a second World War. More than many others of the 20th century, the decade created for itself an identity that gives 'the Thirties' a distinctive character. The decade was an uneasy one in Britain and in the wider world, but the crisis and hardship suffered by many gave rise to literary and other cultural developments that built on the achievements of the earlier years of the century.

In politics, the 1920s had been dominated by the Conservative Party under Stanley Baldwin (1867-1947). The first Labour government was formed under the leadership of Ramsay MacDonald in 1924, but lasted only nine months. For the rest of the decade, Baldwin was Prime Minister, officiating over a period of tranquil but well-judged social reform. In the general election of 1929, Labour unexpectedly took power, albeit dependent on the support of the Liberals, and Ramsay MacDonald formed his second administration. Within months, however, the world economy was devastated by the effects of the Wall Street Crash, caused by the collapse of share prices on the New York Stock Market, which in turn led to the worst ever economic depression experienced by Western economies. The effects of the Great Depression were felt both in the United States and in Europe. This was because, after World War I, the USA had become the main creditor for European countries, particularly Britain and Germany, and from 1929 onwards the supply of loans to Europe dried up as the USA concentrated on supporting its own financial needs.

Unemployment in Britain rose rapidly, affecting 25 per cent of the workforce by 1931. George Orwell wrote in his novel *The Clergyman's Daughter* of 'the great modern commandment – the eleventh commandment which has wiped out all the others: "Thou shalt not lose thy job."' At the same time, there was a run on gold in the banks, as nervous investors sought to guarantee security by taking out their savings in the form of gold bullion. The Labour party was unable to resolve the crisis alone, and so, in August 1931, MacDonald set up a 'national government' by forming a coalition with both the Conservatives and the Liberals. One of the first acts of the new government was to take Britain off the gold standard (the international fixing of currencies to match the value of a certain quantity of gold; see Glossary of Terms) – a deeply unpopular move, but one that was to speed the country's economic recovery. Later that year, a general election was held in which the number of Labour seats was reduced from 288 to 52, and the Conservatives took power with a landslide victory. Nevertheless, MacDonald continued as prime minister and the government remained officially a coalition, since it included so-called National Liberals and National Labour party members.

The parliamentary Labour party considered MacDonald to have betrayed the party, and continued to exist as a separate party, from 1935 under the leadership of Clement Attlee, who was to become prime minister immediately after World War II in 1940.

The Jarrow March

The national coalition government pursued a policy of austerity in order to fight the effects of the depression, keeping tight control over interest rates and encouraging a housing boom and the growth of new industries associated with the consumer age, manufacturing products such as cars and electrical goods. In 1935, Stanley Baldwin replaced the ailing Ramsay MacDonald as prime minister, and the general election of that year confirmed the Conservatives' supremacy, although the government continued to be formed of a coalition of all three main parties. By the mid-1930s, relative prosperity had returned to the south of the country, but Wales and the northeast and northwest of England continued to suffer catastrophic poverty as the depression hit traditional heavy industries such as shipbuilding and coal mining. In Jarrow, on Tyneside, for example, unemployment was as high as 60 per cent, and in 1936 the unemployed men of the city marched from Jarrow to London to bring their desperate state of affairs to the attention of the country and the capital. The march was encouraged by Ellen Wilkinson, the local Labour MP, and in her book *The Town that was Murdered* (1939) she recorded the conditions on Tyneside in the early 1930s, and gave a full account of the journey of the 'hunger marchers':

> On Monday morning the men lined up for a final review by the Mayor outside the Town Hall. The men had done their best to look smart on the little they had. Faces carefully shaved but so thin. Broken boots mended and polished. Shabby clothes brushed and mended by their wives. The waterproof cape rolled over the shoulder bandolier fashion. We marched to Christ Church for a short service, which the men's wives and the Mayor and Corporation attended.

Although the marchers gathered much public support on their way south, little was done or achieved by the government to improve conditions in these depressed areas. The hunger march served only to point up the difference in standards between the north and the south.

Appeasement

When Baldwin resigned as prime minister in 1937, he was succeeded by Neville Chamberlain. The new premier was faced with the challenge of increasing aggression from Fascist dictators in Europe. As Chancellor of the Exchequer, Chamberlain had presided over the recovery from the effects of the Great Depression, and his unwillingness to spend money on rearmament to counteract the massive arms build-up in Germany was coupled with a conviction that the threat presented by Hitler and Mussolini to Europe could be averted through diplomacy and negotiation. In the mid-1930s, Britain deliberately avoided confrontation in various Fascist acts of aggression: the Italian invasion of Ethiopia, the German annexation of the Rhineland, the Spanish Civil War (see page 71), the annexation of Austria into Germany and the occupation of Sudetenland (the part of Czechoslovakia bordering Germany).

By pursuing this policy, which he named 'appeasement', Chamberlain believed that in granting some of Hitler's demands for territory, the stability of the rest of Europe could be guaranteed. In the period from 1938 to the outbreak of war in September 1939, Chamberlain and his Foreign Secretary, Lord Halifax, were involved in a series of negotiations with Hitler, (referred to as the 'Munich crisis') at Berchtesgaden and then at Munich, intended to secure the independence of part of Czechoslovakia and subsequently Poland, in order to avoid a European war. The occupation of Prague in March 1939, the announcement of a pact with Russia in August 1939, and the invasion of Poland in September 1939 exposed the weakness of this policy of appeasement, and Chamberlain fell from power, to be replaced by Winston Churchill.

The Fascist dictators

World War II broke out as a result of the Fascist dictatorships of Adolf Hitler in Germany and Benito Mussolini in Italy. General Francisco Franco was the leader of a Fascist regime in Spain that

—THE ABDICATION CRISIS—

George V died in January 1936 after 26 years on the throne. He was succeeded by his eldest son, Edward VIII, a socialite bachelor, whose current mistress was Wallis Simpson, an American divorcée married to an Englishman. The prime minister, Baldwin, had been told by the then Prince of Wales that Wallis Simpson was in the process of a second divorce from Edward Simpson, and that once it had been completed he intended to marry her. The relationship between the Prince of Wales and Mrs Simpson was unknown to the wider public: in those days the media was very respectful of the royal family's privacy. Baldwin was insistent that the king could not marry Mrs Simpson, because, as king, he was also the head of the Church of England (which forbade divorce to all but a few of its members). It was, therefore, inconceivable that the king should marry a woman twice divorced (and an American). Baldwin gave an ultimatum to Edward that if he did decide to marry Mrs Simpson he would have to abdicate his throne. Matters came to a head in December 1936, when a remark by the Bishop of Bradford that the king would need God's grace in his calling exposed the truth of the crisis. On 11 December, the king made a radio broadcast announcing his decision to abdicate. George V's younger son, the Duke of York, who had never expected to suffer the responsibility suddenly thrust upon him, was crowned George VI in May 1937. The supportive and stoical role that he and his wife, Queen Elizabeth, played in World War II was one that Edward VIII was unlikely to have done. Edward was given the title of the Duke of Windsor, and played various ambassadorial roles overseas until his death in 1972.

The launching of HMS Ark Royal, Birkenhead, April 1937

The aircraft carrier HMS *Ark Royal* was the first major warship to have been built since World War I, and her completion was indicative of the rearmament programme that had slowly gained momentum in the mid 1930s at the instigation of Winston Churchill and Neville Chamberlain. The main threat was expected to come from the air, however, and both the Royal Navy and the Army were severely under-resourced when World War II broke out.

came to power in the aftermath of the Spanish Civil War (see page 71), but although he used military assistance from both Hitler and Mussolini during the civil war, Spain remained neutral during World War II and Franco held on to power until his death in 1975.

The word 'Fascist' comes from an Ancient Roman symbol of state power which Mussolini adopted when he established the Italian Fascist movement in 1919. Fascist regimes shared certain characteristics: the absolute rule of a dictator through a single-party political system; the total subservience of personal concerns to the needs of the state; a strong emphasis on military values, and the use of force and violence to carry out the will of the party; a lack of respect for liberal values and democratic principles; and a strong appeal to nationalist feelings. Fascism was not ultimately concerned with social or political principles, but simply the acquisition and maintenance of power, and in this respect Hitler and Mussolini were not very different from Stalin, who had held power in the Soviet Union, ostensibly in the interests of the Communist state, since 1922. In many of the fictional presentations of such dictatorships, such as the rule of terror of Big Brother in Orwell's novel *Nineteen Eighty-Four* (1949) the distinction between Fascism and Communism is immaterial.

The Italian Fascists were never very popular in Italy as a whole – the country was impatient with badly-run government, heavy national debt in the aftermath of World War I, and the lack of proper state institutions. But in 1922 they marched on Rome and demanded power from the king. This was granted, and within a year Mussolini had outlawed all other political parties, and ruled Italy as a one-party state by means of terror and thuggery carried out by the black-shirted members of the party.

Germany emerged from World War I crippled with debt both from its own war effort, and as a result of the compensation (known as 'reparations') it was forced to pay by the victorious nations. Adolf Hitler, who had served in the German army during World War I, started a political career in the 1920s in the National Socialist Party, (in German, the abbreviation of the party's name – Nazional-sozialistische Deutsche Arbeiterpartein – was Nazi). Through the well-judged use of propaganda in the popular press, mass meetings, and the development of a private army of ex-war veterans, Hitler quickly built up the party. Although an attempt to seize control of the state of Bavaria in 1923 was unsuccessful, by 1930 the Nazi party had become the second largest in the country, and in 1933 Hitler was appointed Chancellor of the German Republic (equivalent to the British prime minister). Having acquired power through more or less legitimate means, Hitler consolidated his position as an absolute dictator. When the German president, Paul von Hindenburg, died in 1934, Hitler merged the offices of president and chancellor, and in the next few years pursued his own personal goals of expanding Germany's borders through armed aggression; destroying Bolshevism and other forms of Socialism in Germany; re-igniting the war against France; and purging Germany of inferior races and social undesirables (as he saw them).

While steadily re-arming and pushing at the post-war borders, Hitler managed to convince the other European powers that he had purely peaceful intentions, and that he was an ally with them against the threat of Socialism. By the time of the invasion of Poland on 1 September 1939, Hitler was prepared to go to war with Britain and France, confident that his tactics would allow him to defeat those two allies quickly in order then to turn his attentions to the East, where he intended to acquire *Lebensraum* ('living space') for the ever-expanding German Reich (empire).

The Spanish Civil War

The Spanish Civil War was perhaps the defining event of the '30s in its impact on British culture. By the mid-1930s, Spanish political and social life had become increasingly split between the right wing, consisting of the Catholic Church, landowners and the armed forces, and the anti-Church left wing, supported by industrial and rural workers and by the middle classes. In February 1936 a left-wing coalition government was brought to power in the general election, but in July of that year a military revolt against the government broke out across the country. Civil war followed shortly afterwards, and within a short time the whole country was divided between rebel, Nationalist areas and government, Republican ones. General Francisco Franco took command of the rebels and in October 1936, was declared head of the new Nationalist state. In 1937 he made the *Falange*, the Spanish Fascist Party, the official party of government, although the Republican government continued to rule its own territory until 1939, when it was forced into exile.

The fighting and civilian violence of the civil war was passionate, but neither side was obviously stronger than the other, and the major European powers were soon implicated in the fighting. Italy and Germany both gave considerable quantities of supplies and personnel to the Nationalists, while the Soviet Union bolstered the Republican forces. Britain and France refused to intervene in the war, but many civilians from these, and many other 'neutral' countries, joined the International Brigade, formed of volunteers willing to fight for the elected socialist government against the Fascist enemy. About 40,000 foreigners fought in the International Brigade, and another 20,000 drove ambulances, served in hospitals or provided other forms of medical, non-combatant support. As was the case at the outbreak of World War I, popular opinion in Britain was divided about the Spanish Civil War, but on the whole the younger generation – inspired with enthusiasm for Communist ideals but ignoring the atrocities that had already happened under Stalin's regime in the name of Communism – supported the Republicans, while older, more established figures supported the Nationalists, again overlooking the brutality that was taking place across Europe in the name of Fascism.

In November 1936, the Nationalists besieged Madrid but were unable to take the capital. In the course of the next two years they gradually gained control of more territory and split the Republican forces in two. At the end of 1938 a large proportion of the government forces were forced into Catalonia in the northeast of the country, from where they crossed the border into France for refuge. In March 1939 fighting broke out between the Republican factions within Madrid and the city fell to the Nationalists by the end of the month. The number of those killed in the civil war is not clear-cut; many civilians were assassinated or died in aerial bombardment, but the final figure lies somewhere between 500,000 and 1,000,000 fatalities. It served as a brutal precursor to World War II, a testing ground for the military activities of Fascists and Communists alike, and a destabilising factor in Europe just when Britain and France were trying to avoid confrontation with Hitler and Mussolini.

One of the best accounts in English is George Orwell's autobiographical record *Homage to Catalonia*, which describes his time fighting with a far-left militia force from 1936 to 1937, when he was shot in the throat. He was discharged from hospital to learn that the Communist militia he had fought for had been declared to be a 'Fascist' organisation, and he had to escape detection and make his way back to England. In the course of the fighting Orwell discovered that the infighting among the Republican forces was as deadly as that against the Fascists. In a letter of July 1937 he wrote:

> I am rather glad to have been hit by a bullet because I think it will happen to us all in the near future and I am glad to know that it doesn't hurt to speak of. What I saw in Spain did not make me cynical but it does make me think that the future is pretty grim. It is evident that people can be deceived by the anti-Fascist stuff exactly as they were deceived by the gallant little Belgium stuff [in the lead up to World War I], and when war comes will walk straight into it... I still think one must fight for Socialism and against Fascism, I mean physically with weapons. Only it is as well to discover which is which.

Volunteers leaving Madrid for the north through cheering crowds, 29 July 1936
The Spanish Civil War broke out in July 1936, when a right-wing military uprising took control of a broad strip of territory in Northern Spain. Pro-government militias headed north to defend Madrid and the heart of the country. The heady and chaotic atmosphere of the early stages of the Spanish Civil War is apparent in this photograph.

—Poetic responses to the Spanish Civil War—

As was the case in World War I, the Spanish Civil War inspired a significant response among the young writers of the time, including Cecil Day Lewis (1904-72), Christopher Isherwood (1904-86), W. H. Auden (1907-73) and Stephen Spender (1909-95). Some saw action and were killed: these included Christopher Caudwell (1901-37) whose Studies in a Dying Culture *(1938) provides interesting analysis of George Bernard Shaw, D.H. Lawrence and T.E. Lawrence (Lawrence of Arabia); Julian Bell (1908-37), nephew of Virginia Woolf; and John Cornford (1915-36), killed on his 21st birthday, who came from a distinguished academic family in Cambridge (he was descended from both Wordsworth and Charles Darwin). The civil war in Spain was seen by many young men and women of the time as a great cause, an ideological conflict between the forces of Socialism and Fascism. Although the memory of World War I was not so distant for some writers, for others such as Cornford, born after the Armistice, the conflict brought out a passion and idealism comparable to that felt by Brooke and others in 1914 (see page 22). In 'Full Moon at Tierz: Before the Storming of Huesca' (written 1936) Cornford wrote:*

Now the same night falls over Germany
And the impartial beauty of the stars
Lights from the unfeeling sky
Oranienburg and freedom's crooked scars.
We can do nothing to ease that pain
But prove the agony was not in vain.

England is silent under the same moon,
From the Clydeside to the gutted pits of Wales.
The innocent mask conceals that soon
Here, too, our freedom's swaying in the scales.
O understand before too late
Freedom was never held without a fight.

Freedom is an easily spoken word
But facts are stubborn things. Here, too, in Spain
Our fight's not won till the workers of all the world
Stand by our guard on Huesca's plain
Swear that our dead fought not in vain,
Raise the red flag triumphantly
For Communism and for liberty.

By contrast, the opening of Spender's 'Two Armies' (1939) is bitter and detached:

Deep in the winter plain, two armies
Dig their machinery, to destroy each other.
Men freeze and hunger. No one is given leave
On either side, except the dead, and wounded.
These have their leave; while new battalions wait
On time at last to bring them violent peace.

Another record of the war can be found in Picasso's painting *Guernica* (1937), commissioned by the Republican government in response to the surprise bombing of a Basque village by German aeroplanes on a busy market day in September 1937. The gored horse, dismembered heads and limbs, and women looking vainly upwards for help commemorate the agony of the occasion, but also serve as a protest against barbarity and inhumanity in general.

Novels of the 1930s

W.H. Auden described the 1930s as 'a low, dishonest decade'. The major novelists of the period, it is true, concentrated on the sordid and depressing side of life. Graham Greene's *Brighton Rock* (1938) tells the story of Pinkie, a youthful gangster in charge of a pathetic collection of crooks who gradually loses power to the organised and sophisticated Colleoni. Pinkie's love for a tea-room waitress called Rose is complicated by his disgust with sex and a residual sense of the importance of his Catholic religion. There is no redemption for Pinkie or for Rose at the end of the novel, as it ends on a note of extreme despair. The last scene shows Rose taking confession; the priest tells her:

> 'I mean – a Catholic is more capable of evil than anyone. I think perhaps – because we believe in Him – we are more in touch with the devil than other people. But we must hope,' he said mechanically, 'hope and pray.'
> 'I want to hope,' she said, 'but I don't know how.'

George Orwell's pre-war novels take as their central characters men who are living lives without direction or joy. *Keep the Aspidistra Flying* (1936) and *Coming up for Air* (1939) both treat the sense of entrapment in the contemporary world: their main characters, Gordon Comstock and George Bowling, are unremarkable, mediocre men looking for something special in their lives and who settle for less when they cannot achieve it. Orwell was a journalist as much as a novelist, and his social writing is similarly concerned with the ordinary people affected by the malaise of the times. *Down and Out in Paris and London* (1933) and *The Road to Wigan Pier* (1937) record his experiences among the workers of the northeast of England, and the labourers and beggars of London and Paris. Despite their preoccupation with the underside of life, nearly all of the major writers of the '30s were themselves comfortably off, well-educated and of a different class from the people about whom they wrote. The writing of Orwell – educated at Eton before joining the Indian Imperial Police in Burma – has been criticised for sentimentalising the working class and presenting a patronising view of their lifestyle. In the following extract from *Keep the Aspidistra*

Flying Gordon Comstock and his friend Ravelston have gone into a 'low-looking pub on a corner in a side-street'. Ravelston considers himself a Socialist, but finds it hard to relate to the workers' own environment:

> Pubs are genuinely proletarian. In a pub you can meet the working class on equal terms – or that's the theory, anyway. But in practice Ravelston never went into a pub unless he was with somebody like Gordon, and he always felt like a fish out of water when he got there... A navvy leaning on the bar turned on his elbow and gave him a long, insolent stare. 'A – toff!' he was thinking. Gordon came back balancing two pint glasses of dark common ale. They were thick, cheap glasses, thick as jam jars almost, and dim and greasy. A thin yellow froth was subsiding on the beer.

Orwell is mocking Ravelston's affected Socialism, but the working-class world is implicated in the mockery as well.

Evelyn Waugh, also educated at public school and Oxford, wrote about his own world in a series of comic novels that satirised the attitudes and follies of the intellectual and upper classes. *Vile Bodies* (1930) dissects the world of post-Oxford socialites – 'bright young things' living a life of parties and worthless activities in Mayfair; in *Black Mischief* (1932) and *Scoop* (1938) he drew on his own experiences as a journalist in Africa in the 1920s. Both novels show the grotesque and self-interested behaviour of white Europeans, accentuated by virtue of their being abroad. As in Orwell's writing (or that of Huxley in *Brave New World*; see page 63), the characters and the situations are subordinate to the satire, and the writing is often strongly non-realistic in its style. Waugh was a comic writer, but in keeping with the times his humour was often bleak and dark.

Many writers of the 1930s were aware of the threat of war that clouded the times. George Bowling in Orwell's *Coming up for Air* returns to the village in which he grew up as a boy, but finds that it has changed radically:

> I started out, but I'd got no further than the market-place when I was pulled up by something I hadn't expected to see. A procession of about fifty school-kids was marching down the street in column of fours – quite military they looked – with a grim-looking woman marching alongside of them like a sergeant-major. The leading four were carrying a banner with a red, white and blue border and BRITONS PREPARE on it in huge letters...
> 'What do they want to march them up and down for?' I said to the barber.

'I dunno. I s'pose it's kind of propaganda, like.'
I knew, of course. Get the kids war minded. Give us all the feeling that there's no way out of it, the bombers are coming sure as Christmas, so down to the cellar you go and don't argue. Two of the great black planes from Walton were zooming over the eastern end of the town. Christ! I thought, when it starts it won't surprise us any more than a shower of rain. Already we're listening for the first bomb.

In her posthumous novel *Between the Acts* (1941), Virginia Woolf reflected on the ending of an age. Begun in April 1938 and completed in March 1941 shortly before Woolf committed suicide, the novel is set in June 1939. The characters are preparing for a village pageant, apparently oblivious to the impending war. After the pageant has taken place and life returns to 'normal', one of the characters, Lucy resumes her reading of her 'Outline of History', which Woolf uses to point up the lack of progress from prehistoric to modern times since the basic human instincts of sex and fighting are as untamed as ever:

'Prehistoric man,' she read, 'half-human, half ape, roused himself from his semi-crouching position and raised great stones.'...
The old people had gone up to bed. Giles crumpled the newspaper and turned out the light. Left alone together for the first time that day, they were silent. Alone, enmity was bared; also love. Before they slept, they must fight; after they had fought they would embrace. From that embrace another life might be born. But first they must fight, as the dog fox fights with the vixen, in the heart of darkness, in the fields of night.
Isa let her sewing drop. And Isa too stood against the window. The window was all sky without colour. The house

—BRITISH SCULPTURE—

Abstract art began to flourish in Britain in the 1920s, largely as the result of the work of Ben Nicholson (1894-1982), Henry Moore (1898-1986) and Barbara Hepworth (1903-75). Nicholson was an artist, influenced first by Picasso and the Cubists (see page 48), and then by the Dutch abstract painter Piet Mondrian (1872-1944). In 1928 Nicholson discovered the naïve, primitive paintings of Alfred Wallis (1855-1942), a fisherman living in St Ives in Cornwall, and established a group of artists in St Ives, which took its name from the town. Nicholson developed a cool, austere tone for his paintings, characterised by circles and rectangles in relief, often relying on white expanses for their effect.

Nicholson married the sculptor Barbara Hepworth, who by the early 1930s had moved to an entirely abstract approach in her work, which gives the impression of being wholly organic, so rounded and smoothed is it that there is often little sense of its having been chiselled. These two, together with Paul Nash established a movement called Unit One, designed to bring international developments to the attention of the British public. But whereas Nicholson and Hepworth were drawn towards abstract art, Nash favoured Surrealism (see page 50), and these became the two twin tracks of British art in the period.

The sculptor Henry Moore was another member of Unit One, and like Hepworth, his work had become entirely abstract by the 1930s. Although his work met with very mixed reactions, he (together with Hepworth) became the most influential British sculptor of the human form in the 20th century. During World War II, Moore turned to drawing as materials for sculpting became scarce, and his drawings of people sheltering from the blitz in Underground stations became one of the lasting images of the war in London.

---

had lost its shelter. It was night before roads were made, or houses. It was the night that dwellers in caves had watched from some high place among the rocks.

The poetry of the 1930s

The link between the advance of the machine age celebrated by the Vorticists and Futurists (see page 48) and the imminence of war became one of the features of poetry of the '30s. W.H. Auden was the leading poet of the time, using his work in a politically conscious way (he was influenced by Marx and Freud) to draw attention to such public themes as the rise of Fascism, unemployment and the industrial depression, and the march of technology and consumerism. He came from a well-to-do background and went to Oxford University to study biology, changing to English once he was there. His interest in science and psychoanalysis can be seen in the observational, analytical quality of his poetry, although the breadth of his interests in languages, history, politics and other pursuits is evident from his writing. In the 1930s, when he submitted his work for publication by the publishers Faber and Faber, T.S. Eliot was the poetry editor there, and the influence of Eliot can also be seen in Auden's spare, economic style, evident in the first stanza of 'Our Hunting Fathers':

> Our hunting fathers told the story
>   Of the sadness of the creatures,
> Pitied the limits and the lack
>   Set in their finished features;
> Saw in the lion's intolerant look,
>   Behind the quarry's dying glare,
> Love ravaging for the personal glory
>   That reason's gift would add,
> The liberal appetite and power,
>   The rightness of a god.

Auden made friends with other young poets while at Oxford in the 1920s. These were Cecil Day Lewis, Louis MacNeice (1907-63) and Stephen Spender, and by the early 1930s they had formed a recognisable literary group, sharing ideas and concerns, usually linked to their support for the Communist party. Other members,

—AUDEN AND BRITTEN—

The composer Benjamin Britten (1913-76) worked closely with many writers and artists in his choral works and operas. He started his musical studies early, and in the 1930s wrote the music for two documentary/propaganda films produced by the GPO [General Post Office] Film Unit, Coalface *(1935) and* Night Mail *(1936). The script for both films was in verse written by Auden, and the two men collaborated on a number of other projects including the song cycle* Our Hunting Fathers *(1936), the operetta* Paul Bunyan *(1941), and the unaccompanied choral setting* Hymn to St Cecilia *(1942). 'Anthem for St Cecilia's Day', as Auden entitled the original poem, explores the relationship between childhood innocence and the sadness and pain that experience necessarily brings:*

> *O cry created as the bow of sin*
> *Is drawn across our trembling violin.*
> *O weep, child, weep, O weep away the stain.*
> *O law drummed out by hearts against the still*
> *Long winter of our intellectual will.*
> *That what has been may never be again.*
> *O flute that throbs with the thanksgiving breath*
> *Of convalescents on the shores of death.*
> *O bless the freedom that you never chose.*
> *O trumpets that unguarded children blow*
> *About the fortress of their inner foe.*
> *O wear your tribulation like a rose.*

_____

connected through school or university links, included the novelists Christopher Isherwood – author of *Mr Norris Changes Trains* (1935) and *Goodbye to Berlin* (1939) on which the musical *Cabaret* was based – and Rex Warner (1905-86). Collaboration between writers was a feature of this group. Auden and Isherwood wrote three plays together including *The Ascent of F6* (1936), Auden and MacNeice travelled to Iceland in 1937, producing the poetic miscellany *Letters from Iceland* on their return, and Isherwood and the novelist Edward Upward (born 1903) created a fantasy world called Mortmere while they were at Cambridge together.

In 1932 an anthology appeared, entitled *New Signatures*. This was conceived by Michael Roberts (1902-48) and John Lehmann (1907-87), two more young writers in the same vein as the Auden group, and published by the Woolfs' Hogarth Press. It contained the work of many poets of the new generation. In some ways its objective was the same as Edward Marsh's *Georgian Poetry* (see page 17): to define a new movement by presenting its output in an anthology in which the reader could make connections and see similarities of style and content for him or herself. As editor, Roberts wrote an introduction to *New Signatures*, setting out a kind of manifesto for the new age, from which this extract is taken:

> The writers in this book have learned to accept the fact that progress is illusory, and yet to believe that the game is worth playing; to believe that the alleviation of suffering is good even though it makes possible new sensitiveness and therefore new suffering; to believe that their own standards are no more absolute than those of other people, and yet to be prepared to defend and to suffer for their own standards; to think of the world, for scientific purposes, in terms which make it appear deterministic, and yet to know that a human action may be unpredictable from scientific laws, a new creation.

The concepts mentioned here of progress, suffering, moral standards and science all signal the new direction in which the *New Signature* poets were travelling. There were differences in treatment: Spender and Day Lewis were relatively lyrical in their techniques while MacNeice was closer to the idiom of Yeats than others, but there is a common thread of concern for the future set against the legacy of the past. In the introduction to his next anthology *New Country* (1933) Roberts wrote that 'we grew up under the shadow of war: we have no memory of pre-war prosperity and a settled Europe. To us that tale is text-book history', and the awareness of war and of conflicting ideologies permeates the poetry of the period. In his *Autumn Journal* (1938) Louis MacNeice reflected on the events leading up to the Munich crisis (see page 68) in a visionary way:

Sleep to the noise of running water
   Tomorrow to be crossed, however deep;
This is no river of the dead or Lethe,
   To-night we sleep
On the banks of the Rubicon – the die is cast;
   There will be time to audit
The accounts later, there will be sunlight later
   And the equation will come out at last.

— WORLD WAR II POETRY —

Poetry was not as common a literary response to World War II as it had been in World War I. The novel was the main form, but there are a number of poets remembered chiefly for their war poetry. Keith Douglas (1920-44) was the most promising of these poets, serving in North Africa and then Normandy, where he was killed by a shell in the landings in 1944. His Selected Poems *was published in 1943, and Ted Hughes revived interest in Douglas's work with an edition published in 1964. In his war poems, set in Africa, Douglas often places the pitiful conflict between humans in the context of the unchanging landscape:*

> *The stars are dead men in the sky*
> *who will applaud the way you die:*
> *the easy sun*
> *won't criticize or carp because*
> *after the death of many heroes*
> *evils remain.*
> *(from 'The Offensive 2')*

Alun Lewis (1915-44) was a Welshman who, after a career as an academic and journalist, joined the army despite his pacifist objections to the war. He served in Burma, where he died in 1944, apparently shot accidentally either by himself or his own side. Sidney Keyes (1922-43) is less well known than Douglas or Lewis, but before his death in Tunisia, he was considered among the more promising of his contemporaries.

Dylan Thomas (1914-53) had written and published before the war, but the influence of his Neo-Romantic style began to be apparent from about 1939 onwards. He was excused from military service because of a lung condition, and worked for a film company that made propaganda films. His poem 'A Refusal to Mourn the Death, by Fire, of a Child in London' is a reminder that World War II had its own 'home front':

> *Deep with the first dead lies London's daughter,*
> *Robed in the long friends,*
> *The grains beyond age, the dark veins of her mother,*
> *Secret by the unmourning water*
> *Of the riding Thames.*
> *After the first death, there is no other.*

Conclusion

When World War II broke out in September 1939, it took few people by surprise. It had been anticipated in much of the literature and art of the 1930s, and the Spanish Civil War had given Europe a taste of how the larger war was likely to develop. Some writers left Europe: in January 1939 Auden and Isherwood had left for the United States, where they spent the duration of the war; Britten, too, emigrated to the USA. Others, such as Evelyn Waugh, enlisted in the armed services and recorded their experiences in the rich harvest of novels written in the late '40s and early '50s: Waugh's *Sword of Honour* trilogy, Rex Warner's *The Aerodrome* (1941), Orwell's *Animal Farm* (1945) and *Nineteen Eighty-Four* (1949), Anthony Powell's *Dance to the Music of Time* sequence of 12 novels (1951-75), and Elizabeth Bowen's *The Heat of the Day* (1949), set in London during the blitz. Much of the pre-war literary life dried up for the duration of the war, although some non-combatants continued to write and reflect on the events taking place around them.

Perhaps the most influential works to be written during the war were three of the four poems that make up T. S. Eliot's *Four Quartets,* published as a collection in 1944: 'East Coker' (1940) 'The Dry Salvages' (1941) and 'Little Gidding' (1942). The earliest, 'Burnt Norton', had been written in 1935. The scope of *Four Quartets* goes well beyond the particular concerns of the war, since Eliot was writing about the continuity of cultural values, the power of memory and the value of a sense of time and place. The *Four Quartets* end with a restrained optimism for the future, drawing together the mystical and historical threads that run through the four poems. The tide of war had barely turned in favour of the Allies in 1943, and the poems were widely appreciated for their blend of contemporary concerns and the appeal to a deeper spirituality in difficult times. Having been a mould-breaking poet in 1922 with *The Waste Land*, Eliot was an establishment figure by 1943, but the *Four Quartets* still capture a sense of the vulnerability of the age and the need to cling on to hope and faith in a dark time:

Quick now, here, now, always –
A condition of complete simplicity
(Costing not less than everything)
And all shall be well and
All manner of thing shall be well
When the tongues of flames are in-folded
Into the crowned knot of fire
And the fire and the rose are one.

TIMELINE

Science, technology and other arts	Literature	History
1899 Schoenberg *Verklärte Nacht*	**1899** Yeats *The Wind Among the Reeds*	**1899** Start of Boer War (to 1902)
1900 Freud *The Interpretation of Dreams*		**1900** Founding of Labour Representation Committee (renamed Labour Party 1906) Australia given status of dominion in British Empire
1901 first trans-Atlantic radio transmission	**1901** Kipling *Kim* Moore *Diarmuid and Grania* **1902** Conrad *Heart of Darkness* Lady Gregory *Cuchulain of Muirthemne* Kipling *Just-So Stories* Yeats *Cathleen ni Houlihan*	**1901** Death of Queen Victoria; succeeded by Edward VII
1903 Wright brothers make first powered flight	**1903** Childers *The Riddle of the Sands* James *The Ambassadors* Moore *The Untilled Field*	**1903** Founding of The Women's Social and Political Union
1905 exhibition at Salon d'Automne marks beginning of Fauvist movement Einstein Special Theory of Relativity	**1904** Founding of Abbey Theatre, Dublin Yeats *In the Seven Woods* Barrie *Peter Pan* Lady Gregory *Gods and Fighting Men* Synge *Riders to the Sea* **1905** Start of Bloomsbury Group (to about 1935) Granville-Barker *The Voysey Inheritance* Forster *Where Angels Fear to Tread* Le Queux 'The Invasion of 1910' serialised in the *Daily Mail*	**1904** Entente Cordiale between Britain and France **1905** Founding of Sinn Féin
1906 development of *Dreadnought* battleship		**1906** Liberals win general election Term 'suffragette' is used by *Daily Mail*
1907 beginning of Cubism Picasso *Les Demoiselles d'Avignon*	**1907** Conrad *The Secret Agent* Kipling awarded Nobel Prize for literature Synge *The Playboy of the Western World*	**1907** New Zealand given status of Dominion in British Empire March from Hyde Park in support of 'Votes for Women'
1908 founding of Motion Picture Patents Company mass-production of Model T Ford begins	**1908** Forster *A Room with a View* Wells *The War in the Air*	

1909 Marinetti publishes 'Futurist manifesto'
Schoenberg Three Pieces for piano, Op. 11
1910 Stravinsky *The Firebird*

1911 Stravinsky *Petrushka*

1912 Sinking of the *Titanic*
Schoenberg *Pierrot Lunaire*

1913 Stravinsky *The Rite of Spring*

1914 first edition of *Blast* marks beginning of Vorticist movement
1915 Dadaist movement founded in Zurich

1916 first official war artists in France
1917 founding of Imperial War Museum

1919 first non-stop transatlantic flight

1921 Stopes founds first birth control clinic

1909 Galsworthy *Strife*
Wells *Ann Veronica*
1910 Forster *Howards End*
Yeats *The Green Helmet*

1911 Conrad *Under Western Eyes*
Moore *Hail and Farewell* (to 1914)
1912 first of Marsh's five anthologies entitled *Georgian Poetry* (to 1922)
1913 Bridges appointed Poet Laureate
Lawrence *Sons and Lovers*
Saki *When William Came; A Story of London under the Hohenzollerns*
1914 Joyce *Dubliners*
Shaw *Common Sense about the War; Pygmalion*
1915 Brooke *1914 and other Poems*
Lawrence *The Rainbow*
1916 Joyce *A Portrait of the Artist as a Young Man*
1917 Eliot *Prufrock and Other Observations*
Gurney *Severn and Somme*
Sassoon *The Old Huntsman*

1918 Sassoon *Counter-attack*

1919 Yeats *The Wild Swans at Coole*
Pound *Homage to Sextus Propertius*

1920 Galsworthy *The Skin Game*
Lawrence *Women in Love*
Owen *Poems*
Pound *Hugh Selwyn Mauberley*
E. Thomas *Collected Poems*
1921 Yeats *Michael Robartes and the Dancer*

1910 Liberals win general election
Death of Edward VII; succeeded by George V
1911 Parliament Bill

1912 Home Rule Bill introduced to Parliament

1913 suffragette Emily Davison dies at the Derby

1914 Start of World War I (to 1918)
Home Rule Act passed but suspended

1916 Easter Rising in Dublin

1918 Conscription introduced in Ireland
Representation of the People Act gives vote to married women over 30
1919 Irish National Assembly (Dáil Eireann) meets in Dublin Mansion House
Lady Astor first woman MP in House of Commons
Mussolini founds Italian Fascist movement

1921 Creation of Irish Free State
Civil war in Ireland (to 1923)

	1922 Eliot *The Waste Land* Galsworthy *The Forsyte Saga* Joyce *Ulysses* Lawrence *Fantasia of the Unconscious* Rosenberg *Poems*	**1922** Women admitted to Civil Service Mussolini leads Fascist march on Rome
1923 Schoenberg Piano Pieces Op. 23	**1923** Yeats awarded Nobel Prize for Literature Lawrence *Kangaroo* O'Casey *The Shadow of a Gunman*	**1923** Matrimonial Causes Act
1924 Breton publishes Surrealist Manifesto	**1924** Forster *A Passage to India* O'Casey *Juno and the Paycock*	**1924** first Labour government
1925 Gropius builds Bauhaus in Dessau	**1925** Woolf *Mrs Dalloway*	
	1926 Lawrence *The Plumed Serpent* O'Casey *The Plough and the Stars*	**1926** General Strike
1927 Spencer murals in Sandham Memorial Chapel, Burghclere, Berkshire (to 1932)	**1927** Woolf *To The Lighthouse*	
1933 founding of Unit One	**1928** Blunden *Undertones of War* Hall *The Well of Loneliness* Lawrence *Lady Chatterley's Lover* published privately Sassoon *Memoirs of a Fox-Hunting Man* Waugh *Decline and Fall* Woolf *Orlando*	**1928** Representation of the People Act gives equal voting rights to men and women
1934 Nicholson meets Mondrian in Paris	**1929** Aldington *Death of a Hero* Galsworthy *A Modern Comedy* Graves *Goodbye to all That*	**1929** Wall Street Crash in New York Start of Great Depression
	1930 Sassoon *Memoirs of an Infantry Officer* Waugh *Vile Bodies*	
	1931 Woolf *The Waves*	**1931** MacDonald forms 'national coalition government'
	1932 Galsworthy awarded Nobel Prize for Literature Huxley *Brave New World* Roberts and Lehmann anthology *New Signatures* Waugh *Black Mischief*	**1933** Hitler becomes Chancellor of Germany
	1933 Brittain *Testament of Youth* Orwell *Down and Out in Paris and London* Roberts anthology *New Country*	
	1934 Waugh *A Handful of Dust*	

1935 Nicholson *White Relief*	**1935** Eliot *Murder in the Cathedral* Isherwood *Mr Norris Changes Trains* Orwell *The Clergyman's Daughter*	
1936 Britten *Our Hunting Fathers*	**1936** Auden and Isherwood *The Ascent of F6* Eliot *Collected Poems 1909-1935* Orwell *Keep the Aspidistra Flying* Sassoon *Sherston's Progress*	**1936** Death of George V; succeeded by Edward VIII Jarrow to London march Spanish Civil War (to 1939) Abdication crisis; George VI becomes king
1937 Picasso *Guernica*	**1937** Auden and MacNeice *Letters from Iceland* Orwell *The Road to Wigan Pier*	**1937** Chamberlain becomes prime minister; starts policy of appeasement
	1938 Caudwell *Studies in a Dying Culture* Greene *Brighton Rock* Orwell *Homage to Catalonia* Waugh *Scoop*	**1938** Hitler annexes Austria Munich agreement
1939 Hepworth and Nicholson move to St Ives	**1939** Isherwood *Goodbye to Berlin* Joyce *Finnegans Wake* Orwell *Coming up for Air* Wilkinson *The Town that was Murdered*	**1939** Hitler invades Poland Start of World War II (to 1945) Churchill becomes prime minister
1940 Moore works as official war artist (to 1942) **1941** Britten *Paul Bunyan* **1942** Britten *Hymn to St Cecilia*	**1940** Greene *The Power and the Glory* **1941** Warner *The Aerodrome* Woolf *Between the Acts* **1943** Douglas *Selected Poems* **1944** Eliot *Four Quartets* **1945** Orwell *Animal Farm* Waugh *Brideshead Revisited*	**1940** Fall of France Evacuation from Dunkirk **1941** Japanese attack Pearl Harbor United States enters war **1944** D-day invasion of France **1945** Atomic bombs dropped on Japan

GLOSSARY OF TERMS

anthropology the study of different civilisations and the development of humans and human behaviour.

appeasement a policy of diplomacy and negotiation towards hostile states in an attempt to avoid war. The term is often used to describe the position taken by Britain towards Germany during the 1930s, when the British prime minister, Neville Chamberlain, deliberately avoided confrontation with the German Chancellor, Adolf Hitler, over acts of aggression.

atonality describes music that is written without reference to a specific key. It was pioneered by the Austrian composer Arnold Schoenberg.

Communism a political philosophy based on the principle that all property should be owned collectively, and that private ownership of property should be abolished. The founder of modern Communism was Karl Marx, who saw Communism as the historical successor to capitalism.

Conservative the most right-wing of the three main British political parties. At the end of the 19th and the start of the 20th century the Conservative party was strongly in favour of maintaining the British Empire and preserving the union with Ireland.

Cubism a movement in art that started in about 1907 and was pioneered by the Spanish artist Pablo Picasso and the French artist Georges Braque. It marked one of the turning-points in the history of Western art, and pointed the way to abstraction. Picasso and Braque rejected the use of conventional perspective, instead dismembering objects and painting them from multiple viewpoints.

Dadaism (from the French meaning 'rocking horse') a movement in art that arose out of disillusion with World War I. It was started in 1915 in Zurich by a group of artists and writers including the artists Jean Arp and Marcel Duchamp and the poet Tristan Tzara. It attacked traditional artistic values, emphasising the absurd and the illogical.

Dáil Eireann the name of the lower house of the Irish parliament. The Dáil was set up in 1919 as a representative assembly while Ireland was still officially ruled from Westminster, and was the first one since the Act of Union of 1800. Its position was formalised by the Anglo-Irish Treaty of 1921, which created the Irish Free State.

dominion the name for certain members of the British Empire: Canada, Australia, New Zealand, South Africa, Eire and Newfoundland which were granted political independence from Great Britain by the Imperial Conference of 1926. The status of the Dominions was given legal confirmation in the Statute of Westminster of 1931. The term was discontinued in 1947, when the term 'member of the Commonwealth' was applied to all former British colonies.

Fascism a political ideology current in Europe in the 1920s and '30s, based on extreme nationalism and authoritarian rule. Fascism raised the role of the dictator to the level of a personality cult, and pursued racist and anti-democratic methods to secure power.

Fauvism (from the French 'les fauves' meaning 'wild beasts') a movement in art that started in 1905 and which experimented with the use of non-naturalistic vivid colour. The main artist in this movement was the French artist Henri Matisse.

Feminism a broad movement that seeks to achieve equal rights and status in society for men and women. The suffragette movement was one of the early forms of feminism in Britain.

Fianna Fáil ('Soldiers of Destiny') the name of the Republican political party founded by Eamon de Valera in protest at the Anglo-Irish Treaty of 1921. The party was formally constituted in 1926, and its members initially refused to swear the oath of allegiance to the British crown and so were unable to sit in the *Dáil*. In 1927, De Valera and his fellow Fianna Fáil members took the oath and rapidly gained political power over the next few years.

figurative a representation in words or art that is non-literal or not strictly representational of the object being depicted. In writing, figurative language departs from the standard meaning or use of words to create a special meaning or effect. Similes and metaphors are common examples of figurative language.

free trade a term used in economics to describe the practice of allowing open and equal trading between countries, without tariffs or trade barriers imposed on goods from certain countries. Britain created its own trading system within its Empire, imposing duties on imported goods in order to protect its own market.

Futurism a modernist art movement that glorified the strength of the machine, the totality of war, the ecstasy of speed and the aggressive advance of the industrial present. Filippo Marinetti founded Futurism in 1909, and its style was generally derived from *Cubism.* It faded around 1918.

Gaelic the native Celtic language of Ireland and the Scottish highlands and islands, and a general term for the traditional culture of the Highlands and Ireland. Although Irish literature survived for a long time as a largely oral culture, Gaelic had died out in Ireland except for some rural areas by the end of the 19th century, and the *Gaelic League* set out to revive the fortunes of the language.

Gaelic League a nationalistic organisation founded by Douglas Hyde in 1893 with the object of reviving Irish traditional language and culture. Many of the leading Irish writers, including W.B. Yeats and J.M. Synge, were involved in the League.

Georgians a group of poets named after a series of five poetry anthologies produced and edited by Edward Marsh from 1912 to 1922. The Georgian poets were largely traditional in their techniques and subject matter, in contrast to the growing trend towards modernism. Some well-regarded writers such as D.H. Lawrence and Edward Thomas had work published in *Georgian Poetry*.

gold standard a monetary system in which the standard unit of currency is a fixed quantity of gold or is kept at the value of a fixed quantity of gold. The currency is freely convertible into a fixed amount of gold per unit of currency. The Wall Street Crash destroyed international confidence in the gold standard, and it was superseded by a system based on paper currencies.

Great Depression the international economic slump caused by the *Wall Street Crash* in October 1929. America stopped making loans to Europe and business confidence suffered a major setback until the mid 1930s.

haiku a traditional form of Japanese poetry, usually describing a natural object or scene in three unrhymed lines of poetry. The first and third lines contain 5 syllables, the second has 7.

Home Rule a term for independent rule, through its own parliament, for Ireland, used in British politics in the late 19th and early 20th centuries. Home Rule did not imply the creation of an independent Irish state, but domestic political freedom within the United Kingdom.

Imagism a poetic movement created by a group of British and American poets that flourished in Britain between 1912 and 1917. Ezra Pound, Amy Lowell, H.D. and William Carlos Williams were among the American writers, D.H. Lawrence and Richard Aldington among the British. The Imagists dispensed with conventions of the 19th century, such as literary formality and the use of regular rhyme and rhythm in poetry, in order to create images that were clear and concentrated.

Irish Free State the political solution to the Anglo-Irish 'War of Independence' from 1919 to 1921. The Irish Free State was granted the status of a *dominion* within the British Empire; six of the counties of Ulster were excluded from the new state and renamed Northern Ireland. The creation of the new state led to civil war that lasted for two years; under the leadership of Eamon De Valera Ireland finally gained full independence in 1937.

Labour one of the three main British political parties in the 20th century. The Labour Party grew out of the trades union movement in the 1890s and was formally constituted in 1900 as the Labour Representation Committee, changing its name to the Labour Party in 1906. It promoted left-wing policies to improve the lives of working people, giving them greater economic, social and political rights.

Liberal one of the three main British political parties. Until the beginning of the 20th century the Liberal Party (which emerged out of the 'Whig' party in the mid-19th century) was the main opposition to the Conservatives, but a series of political mistakes and the rise of support for the *Labour* Party meant that the Liberals held office by themselves for the last time in 1915. Under Herbert Asquith and then David Lloyd George the party took part in a number of coalition governments from 1915 to 1945, but by 1922 it had been overtaken by the Labour Party in popular support.

melodrama a theatrical genre that relies on exaggerated characterisation into types such as the evil villain and the innocent heroine and conventional plot development that relies on suspense and sensationalism.

Modernism a term applied to a range of artistic movements and philosophies that challenged the assumptions about realism behind much of the writing and art of the 19th century. The search for a satisfactory redefinition of form led to radical movements such as Expressionism, Serialism and *Imagism*. The 'high water' period of European modernism is generally taken to run from 1910 to 1930.

myth one of a number of stories with which a culture explains or justifies its cultural and social customs, often involving supernatural or non-human activity or intervention in human affairs. Most myths are linked to social rituals. In literary terms, myths are invoked as fictional stories designed to reveal deeper truths about life, death and religion. A body of myths is known as a mythology.

parody a humorous or satirical imitation of a literary style, which gains its effect through mocking exaggeration of the original's stylistic character.

Postmodernism a term for the cultural phase that followed *Modernism* in the 1950s and afterwards. The characteristics of Postmodernism are difficult to reduce to a simple definition, but include the replacement of representation with self-reference and a highly developed use of irony and self-deprecation. Postmodernism rejects the search for meaning in a work of art, celebrating a wholly subjective approach to meaning and matter.

psychoanalysis the practice of psychology which examines the role of the unconscious in the formation of one's mental life. The interpretation of dreams and the free association of ideas are important in gaining a better understanding of the patient's deeper emotions.

saga originally a traditional tale in Icelandic or Norse literature relating a family or royal history. In its broader sense the word has come to mean a novel or series of novels telling the story of several generations of the same family.

satire writing that exposes the weaknesses and criticises the vices of individuals or institutions. Its method can be gently mocking or bitterly aggressive. Satire can be found in all literary forms, and can be either explicit or implied.

Sinn Féin a nationalist party established in 1905 by Arthur Griffith to promote the cause of Irish independence and encourage civil disobedience against British rule. The name means 'We Ourselves' or 'Ourselves Alone'. The party was initially slow to attract a following but after the Easter Rising in 1916 it rapidly gained popularity and De Valera used his leadership of the party to achieve his political goals in the bitter power struggles in the years between 1916 and 1926, when he split from Sinn Féin and founded the *Fianna Fáil* party.

Socialism a very broad term that describes the political doctrine whereby members of a society put the needs of their society before their own: some degree of social control means that private property and the distribution of income are regulated by the state. Socialism occurs in many forms ranging from liberal socialism to Marxist revolutionary socialism.

stream-of-consciousness originally a term from psychology to describe the random activity of the mind, the expression was applied to the style of writing that attempts to recreate such uncontrolled and subjective mental activity. James Joyce and Virginia Woolf were among the writers to use the technique.

Surrealism a movement in art and literature that started in the 1920s, and which grew out of *Dadaism.* Like Dadaism, it emphasised the irrational and the absurd. However, it also drew on the theories of the Austrian psychoanalyst Sigmund Freud, particularly in relation to the subconscious and the importance of dreams. The French poet André Breton published the first Surrealist Manifesto in 1924. The movement was very influential, particularly through the work of painters such as Max Ernst, Joan Miró, René Magritte and Salvador Dali.

Trades Union Congress an association of trades unions, founded in 1868. Its purpose is to develop and maintain relations with the government and employers, to advance the interests of union members and to mediate in disputes.

Unionist a term used to describe politicians who opposed the Irish independence movement. The Liberal government under William Gladstone proposed to grant *Home Rule* to Ireland, but a breakaway group of Liberals under Joseph Chamberlain combined with the Conservatives to defeat the Bill, calling themselves Liberal Unionists. The Conservative party renamed itself the Conservative and Unionist party in 1909.

Vorticism a brief artistic movement established in 1914 by Wyndham Lewis and linked but opposed to *Futurism.* The main vehicle for its activity was the magazine *Blast*, which appeared for two issues in 1914 and 1915.

Wall Street Crash an American economic crisis that created the *Great Depression* – a ten-year slump that affected all Western economies. The Wall Street Crash was caused by a rapid increase in share prices through the mid-1920s which came to a head in mid-October 1929, when panic selling of shares caused the market to collapse.

BIOGRAPHICAL GLOSSARY

Auden, Wystan Hugh (1907-73) writer and critic. Born in York, he was educated at a prep school in Surrey where he met his lifelong friend, Christopher Isherwood, at Gresham's School in Norfolk and at Oxford University. At university he came into contact with many other literary figures including Stephen Spender, C. Day Lewis and Louis MacNeice. His first volume of poetry was published by Spender in 1928, followed by several more collections in the 1930s. He worked with Isherwood on three plays *The Dog beneath the Skin*, *The Ascent of F6* and *On the Frontier*, and with Louis MacNeice on *Letters from Iceland* after a trip to that country in 1937. In 1935 he married Erika Mann, daughter of the German novelist Thomas Mann, to allow her to escape from Nazi Germany. During the Spanish Civil War he went to Spain to work as an ambulance driver for the Republicans (see page 71). He reported on his experiences in *Spain*. In 1939 he emigrated to the USA and became an American citizen in 1946. In the USA, he met his lifelong partner, Chester Kallman. He became professor of poetry at Oxford University in 1956.

Blunden, Edmund (1896-1974) writer and critic. Born in London, although his family moved soon afterwards to Kent, he was educated at Christ's Hospital and Oxford University. He served in the Royal Sussex Regiment in France during World War I. After the war he went to Japan where he became professor of English Literature in 1924. Other posts included professor of English in Hong Kong (1953), and professor of poetry at Oxford (1966). His early poems were published in *Georgian Poetry* (see page 17), but he is best remembered for his memoir of the war *Undertones of War*. He also wrote biographies of many literary figures, including Leigh Hunt, Percy Bysshe Shelley and Thomas Hardy.

Brittain, Vera (1893-1970) see box page 63
Brooke, Rupert (1887-1915) see box page 22
Conrad, Joseph (1857-1924) see page 15
Day Lewis, Cecil (1904-72) writer and critic. Born in Sligo, Ireland, he was educated at Sherborne School and Oxford University. At university he met W.H. Auden and other literary figures. He published his first collection of poetry in 1925, but established a reputation with *Transitional Poems* in 1929. He was a member of the Communist Party until 1939, and worked for the Ministry of Information during World War II. He was professor of poetry at Oxford from 1951-56 and became Poet Laureate in 1968.

Doyle, Sir Arthur Conan (1859-1930) novelist. Born in Edinburgh, he was educated at Stonyhurst College and went on to study medicine at Edinburgh University. As a young doctor in Plymouth and then Southsea, he began to write to supplement his income. The first Sherlock Holmes novel, *A Study in Scarlet*, appeared in 1887 in *Beeton's Christmas Annual*. *The Sign of Four* was published in 1890. From 1891-3 onwards, *The Adventures of Sherlock Holmes* appeared in *Strand Magazine*, where they achieved huge popularity. When Doyle grew tired of his Sherlock Holmes and attempted unsuccessfully to kill him off, public opinion forced him to revive his hero. Doyle also wrote historical fiction, for example *Micah Clarke* and *The White Company*, as well as science fiction, such as *The Lost World*, *The Poison Belt* and *The Land of Mist*. He served as a doctor in the Boer War, writing *The War in South Africa* which won him a knighthood.

Eliot, Thomas Stearns (1888-1965) writer and critic. Born in St Louis, Missouri, USA, he went to Harvard University before spending a year in Paris, and taking up a scholarship at Oxford University in the UK. He decided to stay in England and became a British citizen in 1927. After a short time teaching, he worked for Lloyds Bank for eight years before becoming a director of the publishing company Faber and Faber. In 1915, he married Vivien Haigh-Wood; after an unhappy marriage they formally separated in 1932-3. Eliot married a second time in 1957, to Valerie Fletcher. Encouraged by Ezra Pound, he published his first volume of poetry *Prufrock and Other Observations* in 1917. He became involved with the Bloomsbury Group, and his next two volumes of poetry were published by Leonard and Virginia Woolf's Hogarth Press. His important work *The Waste Land* appeared in 1922 in the first edition of *The Criterion*, a quarterly review which Eliot edited until 1939. *The Waste Land* quickly became a central text of the Modernist movement. In 1927, Eliot became a member of the Church of England, and his work after this date reflects his religious faith, for example in poems such as 'Ash Wednesday' and the play *Murder in the Cathedral*. The major work of Eliot's later career was *Four Quartets*, published in 1944. In 1948, Eliot was awarded the Nobel Prize for Literature.

Galsworthy, John (1867-1933) novelist and playwright. Born in Surrey, he was educated at Harrow and Oxford University, where he studied law. After university, he decided to travel and become a writer. On one of his trips abroad he met Joseph Conrad, and the two became lifelong friends. His first book was published in 1897, and his first play, *The Silver Box*, produced in 1906. Also in 1906, he published the first of the hugely successful Forsyte Saga novels *The Man of Property*. In his career as a playwright he wrote over 30 plays, including *Strife* and *The Skin Game*, many of which dealt with social injustice. He was awarded the Nobel Prize for Literature in 1932.

Granville-Barker, Harley (1877-1946) actor, producer and playwright. Born in London. He appeared as an actor in George Bernard Shaw's production of his own play, *Candida*, in 1900, and he continued his influential work with Shaw in a series of plays that appeared at the Royal Court Theatre from 1904-7. Granville-Barker's plays include *The Voysey Inheritance*, *Waste* and *The Madras House*.

Graves, Robert von Ranke (1895-1985) writer and critic. Born in London, he was educated at Charterhouse School. He joined up in 1914 and fought on the Western Front in France, where he was badly injured. His first collections of poetry, *Over the Brazier*, *David and Goliath* and *Fairies and Fusiliers* were published during the war; his work also appeared in *Georgian Poetry* (see page 17). After the war, he went to Oxford University, where he became a friend of T.E. Lawrence, of whom he later wrote a biography. He met Laura Riding in 1925, and travelled the world with her, living for a time in Majorca. He returned to England during World War II, but settled permanently in Majorca with his second wife after 1946. He wrote a memoir of World War I, *Goodbye to All That*, as well as many works of criticism, most famously *The White Goddess*. He also published collections of poetry and historical novels such as *I Claudius*. He was professor of poetry at Oxford from 1961-66.

Greene, Graham (1904-91) writer and critic. Born in Berkhamsted, Hertfordshire, and educated at the school there, where his father was headmaster. He went to Oxford University where he published his first collection of poetry *Babbling April* (1925). A key event in his life was his conversion to Roman Catholicism in 1926. In the same year he also joined *The Times* as a journalist. His first successful novel was *Stamboul Train*, published in 1932, followed by many others which Greene labelled 'Entertainments'. Catholicism was examined in his novels *Brighton Rock (1938)*, *The Power and the Glory (1940)*, *The Heart of the Matter (1948)* and *The Quiet American (1955)*. He loved travelling, and published many travel books. He was also film critic for *The Spectator*, and wrote plays for the theatre and the screenplay for the film *The Third Man*.

Gurney, Ivor (1890-1937) see page 23 and box page 26

Huxley, Aldous (1894-1963) novelist. Born in Surrey to a distinguished family, he was educated at Eton and Oxford University. He worked as a journalist, and in 1921 published *Crome Yellow* which established his reputation as a witty and satirical writer. During the 1920s, Huxley lived for a time in Italy where he became friends with D.H. Lawrence, who appears as a character in Huxley's book *Point Counter Point* (1928). His most famous novel was *Brave New World* (see page 63). Huxley suffered from an eye disease which forced him to move to the warmer climate of California, where he settled after 1937.

Isherwood, Christopher (1904-86) novelist and playwright. Born in Cheshire, he met W.H. Auden at a prep school in Surrey, before going to Repton School and Cambridge University. From 1929-33 he was a teacher of English in Berlin, and this period provided the inspiration for his novels *Mr Norris Changes Trains* (1935) and *Goodbye to Berlin* (1939), on which the musical *Cabaret* was later based. He wrote three plays with Auden (see page 79), as well as travelling to China with him, the result of which was *Journey to a War*. In 1939, Isherwood emigrated to the USA with Auden, becoming an American citizen in 1946. He wrote screenplays for the film company Metro-Goldwyn-Mayer, and became increasingly interested in Indian philosophy and religion.

James, Henry (1843-1916) see page 15

Joyce, James (1882-1941) see page 39

Kipling, Rudyard (1865-1936) Poet and novelist. Born in India, he was left as a young child in England with foster parents and sent to school in Devon before working as a journalist in India for seven years. He settled in 1902 in the Sussex countryside, which inspired his later writing. He wrote a number of successful children's stories including *The Jungle Book* and the *Just-So Stories*, as well as a wide range of fiction – novels and short stories – and verse. Dramatic voices and popular forms such as the ballad, hymn or music hall lyric are a characteristic of the poetry published in volumes such as *Departmental Ditties* or *Barrack Room Ballads*. In the early days of the century he enjoyed a high reputation, such that in 1907 he was the first English author to be awarded the Nobel Prize for literature. T.S. Eliot, who was not unselective in his tastes and judgements, rated him highly and edited a selection of his poetry in 1941.

Lawrence, David Herbert (1885-1930) novelist, poet, playwright and critic. Born in Eastwood, Nottinghamshire, his father was a coal miner. From childhood onwards, Lawrence suffered from poor health, mainly illnesses of the lungs. With the encouragement of his mother, he became a school teacher but he was forced to give up teaching after a serious illness. By this time (1911) he had published his first novel, *The White Peacock*, and decided to make his living as a writer. In 1912, he met the wife of one of the professors at Nottingham University, Frieda von Richthofen. The two eloped, and travelled in Europe during 1912 and 1913, getting married in 1914 after Frieda's divorce. Lawrence's semi-autobiographical novel *Sons and Lovers* was published in 1913. During World War I the

Lawrences moved to Cornwall, where they were treated with great suspicion because of Frieda's German nationality. *The Rainbow*, published in 1915, was prosecuted and banned on the grounds of obscenity, and Lawrence was unable to find a publisher for his next novel *Women in Love* until 1920. In 1919, the Lawrences left England for Italy, where they lived for three years before travelling to Australia, Mexico and the USA. These travels provided the settings for novels such as *Kangaroo* (1923) and *The Plumed Serpent* (1926) Lawrence's last novel, *Lady Chatterley's Lover* was published privately in Italy in 1928: it did not appear in its complete form in the UK until 1960. Lawrence also wrote many short stories, poems and non-fiction works.

Lewis, (Percy) Wyndham (1882-1957) artist, writer and critic. Born on a yacht off the east coast of the United States, he was educated at Rugby School and the Slade School of Art in London before spending several years in Paris. With Ezra Pound he started the Vorticist movement and founded its magazine *Blast*, although only two issues were published. During World War I he served on the Western Front in France, first as a soldier and subsequently as a war artist. His first novel *Tarr* was published in 1918. In the 1930s he wrote the satirical novels *The Apes of God*, set in London, and *The Revenge for Love*, set in the Spanish Civil War. At the beginning of World War II, he emigrated to Canada, returning to England in 1945.

MacNeice, Louis (1907-63) poet. Born in Belfast, Ireland, he was educated at Marlborough School and Oxford University. His first volume of poetry, *Blind Fireworks*, was published in 1929. He taught at Birmingham and London universities before starting to work for the BBC in 1941, a post he held until his death. He wrote many programmes and plays for radio, including *The Dark Tower*. He collaborated with Auden on *Letters from Iceland* (see page 79), and was also linked with other literary figures such as Cecil Day Lewis and Stephen Spender.

Moore, George (1852-1933) novelist and playwright. Born in Ballyglass, County Mayo, Ireland, he was educated at Oscott College in Birmingham. His father's death in 1870 gave him the financial independence to study painting and write. He spent several years in Paris, where he published his first two collections of poetry *Flowers of Passion* and *Pagan Poems*. He was influenced by the French novelist Émile Zola, and brought Zola's ideas to a British public in novels such as *A Modern Lover* and *Esther Waters*. He opposed the Boer War, and returned to Ireland in 1899 where he became involved in the Irish literary renaissance (see page 38). After the end of the Boer War, Moore returned to London where he lived for the rest of his life. He published various memoirs including *Hail and Farewell* in which he wrote about the process of setting up the Abbey Theatre in Dublin (see page 36).

O'Casey, Sean (1880-1964) playwright. Born in Dublin, to a poor Protestant family. He worked as a labourer and became involved in the Nationalist movement before starting a career as a playwright. After several rejections from the Abbey Theatre, O'Casey's first success was the play *The Shadow of a Gunman*, produced in 1923. It was followed by *Juno and the Paycock* and *The Plough and the Stars*, which dealt with the Easter Rising and caused the Nationalist audience in Dublin to riot. O'Casey left Ireland for London, where his next play *The Silver Tassie* was staged in 1929. He never lived in Ireland again, continuing to write plays and an autobiography in later life.

Orwell, George (real name Eric Arthur Blair) (1903-50) novelist and journalist. Born in Bengal, India, he was educated at Eton College. He joined the Indian Imperial Police in Burma, resigning in 1927 after five years. He returned to Europe where he took various badly paid jobs in London and Paris, living in some poverty – an experience he described in his first book *Down and Out in Paris and London*. From 1935 he became a country shopkeeper, and it is from this period that the novels *A Clergyman's Daughter* and *Keep the Aspidistra Flying* both date. In 1936, the publisher Victor Gollancz commissioned Orwell to investigate unemployment in the north of England; as a result Orwell produced *The Road to Wigan Pier*. Orwell fought and was wounded in the Spanish Civil War, an experience he described in *Homage to Catalonia*. He worked as a war correspondent for the BBC during World War II. His best-known works, the satires *Animal Farm* and *Nineteen Eighty-Four*, were published in 1945 and 1949 respectively.

Pound, Ezra (1885-1972) see page 54

Rosenberg, Isaac (1890-1918) see page 23

Sackville-West, Vita (1892-1962) poet and novelist. Born at Knole, Kent into an aristocratic family. She started to write plays and books as a child. In 1913 she married the diplomat Harold Nicolson and travelled widely with him. Her first published work, *Poems of West and East*, appeared in 1917, and was followed two years later by the novel *Heritage*. Her reputation as a writer was made with the long poem *The Land*, and she went on to write many more works including an account of her family, *Knole and the Sackvilles*. She was also an expert gardener, working in the gardens of her home at Sissinghurst in Kent, and writing a weekly column on gardening for *The Observer*. She was also a close friend of Virginia Woolf, and provided the model for the hero/heroine of Woolf's *Orlando* (see page 65).

Sassoon, Siegfried (1886-1967) poet and novelist. Born in Kent, he was educated at Marlborough School and Cambridge University. On the outbreak of war in 1914 he joined the Royal Welch Fusiliers and served on the Western Front in France, where he met Robert Graves. He was wounded, and his experiences of the war affected him so deeply that in 1917 he issued 'A Solder's Declaration' asserting that the war was being prolonged deliberately 'by those who have the power to end it'. Graves intervened to save his friend from court-martial, and Sassoon was sent to recover in Craiglockhart Hospital in Edinburgh, where he met Wilfred Owen. He published his first two collections of poems, both deeply anti-war, in 1917 *The Old Huntsman* and 1918 *Counter-Attack*. He returned to the Western Front, but survived the war, and later wrote three prose memoirs of his experiences which were collected in one volume under the title *The Complete Memoirs of George Sherston*.

Shaw, George Bernard (1856-1950) playwright, novelist and critic. Born in Dublin, Ireland, into a Protestant family. His mother was a singing teacher, and from her he inherited a love of music. He left school at 15 and worked briefly for an estate agent before leaving Ireland. He went to London where he read widely, including the works of Karl Marx. He became a Socialist (see Glossary of Terms) and in 1884 joined the Fabian Society (see page 10). He worked as a music and drama critic, and published several novels. In 1898 he married an Irish heiress, Charlotte Payne-Townshend. During the 1890s he also began to write plays, including *Mrs Warren's Profession*, *Arms and the Man* and *Candida*. His fame grew with the influential season at the Royal Court Theatre from 1904-7 (see Granville-Barker) at which plays such as *Man and Superman* and *Major Barbara* were given their first performances. During World War I, Shaw excited controversy with his *Common Sense about the War* (see page 19). He was awarded the Nobel Prize for Literature in 1925.

Spender, Stephen (1909-1995) poet. Born in London, he was educated at University College School and Oxford University. At university he met W.H. Auden and other writers. His first successful collection of poetry was *Poems*, published in 1933. He was in Spain during the Spanish Civil War, and his experiences there are reflected in *Poems from Spain*. During World War II he worked as a fireman in London, publishing more collections of poetry in 1941 (*Runes and Vision* and *Poems of Dedication*). After the war he concentrated more on literary criticism, holding many academic posts both in the UK and in the USA. He was knighted in 1983.

Synge, John Millington (1871-1909) see page 37

Waugh, Evelyn (1903-66) novelist. Born in London, he was educated at Lancing College and Oxford University. After university he became a schoolteacher, and although the experience was not a happy one it provided him with the material for his first successful novel, published in 1928, *Decline and Fall*. In the same year he married Evelyn Gardner, but the marriage was not a success and they were divorced two years later. In 1930, Waugh became a Roman Catholic, an event which was of the utmost importance to him. During the 1930s he became established as a satirical novelist with books such as *Black Mischief*, *A Handful of Dust* and *Scoop*. He married again in 1937, and settled in Gloucestershire with his wife, Laura Herbert. During World War II he was a junior officer in the Royal Marines. He published his most famous book, *Brideshead Revisited*, in 1945, and the three books that make up *The Sword of Honour* trilogy (1965), drew on his war experiences.

Wells, Herbert George (1866-1946) novelist and historian. Born in Kent, the son of an unsuccessful shopkeeper, he left school at 16 to become a draper's apprentice. After two years he became a pupil teacher at Midhurst Grammar School before winning a scholarship to study at the Normal School of Science (now Imperial College) in London. After gaining a degree in zoology in 1890, he decided to become a writer. In the same year he married his cousin, but the marriage failed and they were divorced. He married again in 1895, to Amy Robbins, whom he called Jane. This marriage was successful, although Wells had numerous affairs, including one with the novelist Rebecca West. His first major publication was the science fiction novel *The Time Machine*, published in 1895. Others followed, including *The Island of Dr Moreau* and *The War of the Worlds*. From 1903 he was a member of the Fabian Society, although he argued with many of its members. He also wrote comic novels such as *Kipps* and *The History of Mr Polly*, as well as non-fiction works such as *The Outline of History*, and a warning about the dangers of Fascism, *The Shape of Things to Come*.

Woolf, Virginia (1882-1941) writer and publisher. Born in London, she was educated at home. After the death of her father, Sir Leslie Stephen, in 1904, she moved to Bloomsbury with her sister Vanessa (later Vanessa Bell) and her brothers. This was the first meeting place of the Bloomsbury Group (see page 43). She married Leonard Woolf in 1912, and her first novel *The Voyage Out* was published in 1915. The Woolfs established the Hogarth Press which published works by Katherine Mansfield and T.S. Eliot (notably *The Waste Land*; see page 56) as well as the Woolfs' own writing. Her three greatest novels – *Mrs Dalloway*, *To the Lighthouse* and *The Waves* – confirmed her place in the Modernist movement. However, she suffered from poor health and had many nervous breakdowns. A final illness led her to commit suicide by drowning in 1941.

Yeats, William Butler see page 35

FURTHER READING

1. INTRODUCTION
Clive Bloom (ed.) *Literature and Culture in Modern Britain Volume 1: 1900-1929*, Longman 1993
Peter Clarke *Hope and Glory: Britain 1900-1990*, Penguin 1996
Martin Dodsworth (ed.)*The Penguin History of Literature 7: The Twentieth Century*, Penguin 1994. Poetry, prose and drama are given separate treatment for each phase of the century.
John Lucas *Modern English Poetry from Hardy to Hughes*, Batsford 1986. Includes discussion of Hardy, Kipling and other early 20th century poets.
Robert Rhodes James *The British Revolution; British Politics 1880-1939*, Random House 1977. Politician's interpretation of the history of this period.
Raymond Williams *Drama from Ibsen to Brecht*, Hogarth Press 1993

2. WORLD WAR I
Bernard Bergonzi *Heroes' Twilight: A Study of the Literature of the Great War*, Constable 1965
Simon Featherstone *War Poetry; An Introductory Reader*, Routledge 1995. Includes discussions of various aspects of war poetry throughout the 20th century, a representative selection of familiar and less well-known poems, and prose extracts.
Niall Ferguson *The Pity of War*, Penguin 1998. A detailed but highly readable and individual history of the Great War.
Paul Fussell *The Great War and Modern Memory*, Oxford University Press 1975
Samuel Hynes *A War Imagined; The First World War and English Culture,* Bodley Head 1990
Jon Silkin *Out of Battle*, Oxford University Press 1972

3. IRELAND
Peter Costello *The Heart Grown Brutal; the Irish Revolution in Literature, from Parnell to the Death of Yeats, 1891-1939*, Gill and Macmillan 1977
Una Ellis-Fermor *The Irish Dramatic Movement*, Methuen (2nd ed.) 1954
Richard Ellmann *James Joyce*, Oxford University Press (rev. ed.) 1982
Robert Kee *The Green Flag*, Weidenfeld and Nicholson 1972. A three-volume history of Ireland. The second volume, *The Bold Fenian Men*, covers the period from the 1870s to 1916, and the third, *Ourselves Alone*, deals with events from the Easter Rising to the founding of the Irish Free State.

4. MODERNISM
Malcolm Bradbury and James McFarlane (eds) *Modernism; A Guide to European Literature 1890-1930*, Penguin 1976

Peter Faulkner *A Modernist Reader,* Batsford 1986. Contains a good selection of key documents by the main modernist authors.
Peter Faulkner *Modernism*, Routledge 1977. A useful short guide, in the *Critical Idiom* series.
Hugh Kenner *The Pound Era*, Alfred Knopf 1971
Hugh Kenner *A Sinking Island; the Modern English Writers*, Alfred Knopf 1988. An idiosyncratic but very readable account of the leading Modernists.
Michael Levenson *The Cambridge Companion to Modernism*, Cambridge University Press 1999. Essays cover the main literary genres as well as art, film and gender.

5. WOMEN IN SOCIETY AND LITERATURE (1900-45)
Lucy Bland *Banishing the Beast; English Feminism and Sexual Morality 1885-1914*, Penguin 1995
Sue Bruley *Women in Britain since 1900*, Macmillan 1999
Sheila Rowbotham *A Century of Women; the History of Women in Britain and the United States*, Viking 1977
Claire Tylee *The Great War and Women's Consciousness: Images of Militarism and Feminism in Women's Writings 1914-1964*, Macmillan 1990

6. THE THIRTIES
Bernard Bergonzi *Reading the Thirties*, Macmillan 1978. A selective but acutely observed study of the period.
Gary Day (ed.) *Literature and Culture in Modern Britain Volume 2: 1930-1955*, Longman 1997. A detailed and wide-ranging treatment of popular culture in all its forms as well as the literature of the period.
Samuel Hynes *The Auden Generation; Literature and Politics in England in the 1930s*, Bodley Head 1976
Norman Page *The Thirties in Britain*, Macmillan 1990. Uses literary and contemporary historical accounts to build up a sense of the age.

WEBSITES
The following websites provide gateways for further research into Modernism:

http://newark.rutgers.edu/~jlynch/Lit/20th.html
http://www.bedfordstmartins.com/litlinks/periods/modern.htm
http://www.artsmia.org/modernism/

INDEX